Ray Toal · John David N. Dionisio

Loyola Marymount University

the JAVASCRIPT
Programming Language

JONES AND BARTLETT PUBLISHERS

Sudbury, Massachusetts

BOSTON   TORONTO   LONDON   SINGAPORE

World Headquarters

Jones and Bartlett Publishers
40 Tall Pine Drive
Sudbury, MA 01776
978-443-5000
info@jbpub.com
www.jbpub.com

Jones and Bartlett Publishers
Canada
6339 Ormindale Way
Mississauga, Ontario L5V 1J2
Canada

Jones and Bartlett Publishers
International
Barb House, Barb Mews
London W6 7PA
United Kingdom

Jones and Bartlett's books and products are available through most bookstores and online booksellers. To contact Jones and Bartlett Publishers directly, call 800-832-0034, fax 978-443-8000, or visit our website www.jbpub.com.

Substantial discounts on bulk quantities of Jones and Bartlett's publications are available to corporations, professional associations, and other qualified organizations. For details and specific discount information, contact the special sales department at Jones and Bartlett via the above contact information or send an email to specialsales@jbpub.com.

Production Credits
Acquisitions Editor: Timothy Anderson
Editorial Assistant: Melissa Potter
Production Director: Amy Rose
Production Assistant: Ashlee Hazeltine
Composition: Northeast Compositors, Inc.
Cover Design: Scott Moden
Cover Image and Title Page: © Norebbo/ShutterStock, Inc.
Printing and Binding: Malloy, Inc.
Cover Printing: Malloy, Inc.

Library of Congress Cataloging-in-Publication Data
Toal, Ray.
  The JavaScript programming language / Ray Toal, John David N. Dionisio.
     p. cm.
  ISBN-13: 978-0-7637-6658-0 (pbk.)
  ISBN-10: 0-7637-6658-5 (ibid.)
  1. JavaScript (Computer program language) I. Dionisio, John David N., 1970– II. Title.

QA76.73.J38T63 2009
005.2'762—dc22

                                    2008041381

6048

Printed in the United States of America
13 12 11 10 09   10 9 8 7 6 5 4 3 2 1

Contents

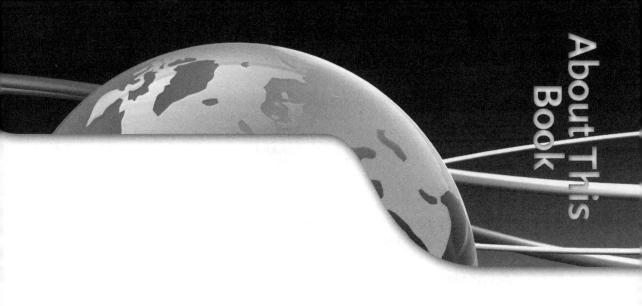

This short guide introduces the JavaScript™ programming language. It is targeted to students taking a general-interest computer science course (CS0) who need material on a specific programming language to complement a language-neutral primary text. For this reason, we limit our coverage to the "good parts" [Cro08a] subset of the JavaScript language. While no previous programming experience is assumed, this guide is fast paced and at times includes material not traditionally presented at the introductory level. Therefore, it is also suitable for seasoned programmers who are new to the language and desire a practical introduction. Sections with advanced material that can be safely skipped are marked with an asterisk (*).

While the book strives to teach basic programming practice, it is ultimately about the JavaScript *language*, and thus includes details of objects, functions, constructors, and prototypes. Understanding a language's structural foundation is necessary to express oneself effectively in that language. Of course, we do not neglect the fact that JavaScript is the primary language for making web browsers more interactive. Given that web programming is only one *application area* of JavaScript, however, we purposely defer coverage of this topic until after much of the language has been covered in detail.

Because the book is concise, it's best read cover to cover. We start with the rationale for the JavaScript language and quickly introduce several short example programs. The middle chapters of the text cover the major elements of the language in a rather technical fashion, illustrated with ready-to-run example code. The last chapter explores JavaScript's use on the World Wide Web, briefly introducing DHTML and Ajax. We encourage readers to enter and run the sample code, and to work through the many exercises at the end of each chapter.

We do hope that readers who have picked up this book only to satisfy a required course in JavaScript will nevertheless gain the knowledge and skills necessary to move on to study the interesting and rewarding disciplines of computer science and software engineering.

Text Website

Visit `http://www.jbpub.com/catalog/9780763766580` for errata, additional exercises, solutions, and more sample code.

Acknowledgments

We are grateful to Loren Abrams, Hervé Franceschi, and B. J. Johnson for their insight and comments; all took significant time and effort to help us improve the text a great deal. Thanks also to Mike Megally and Matt Werner for giving us their overall impressions.

Love and thanks to Mei Lyn, Aidan, Anton, and Aila for their support and perspective. —JDND

Finally, Tim Anderson, Acquisitions Editor; Melissa Potter, Editorial Assistant; Amy Rose, Production Director; Ashlee Hazeltine, Production Assistant; and their Jones and Bartlett colleagues were instrumental in encouraging this book and seeing it through the entire production process.

Introduction

Rather than introducing you to JavaScript, this chapter takes the approach of initiating you into it. After briefly discussing why JavaScript is worth learning, we jump immediately into writing and running a variety of real JavaScript programs.

1.1 Why JavaScript?

JavaScript, which is one of many programming languages that are in use today, is primarily known as the technology that allows web pages to become "dynamic" or "interactive." Every programming language comes with its own merits, distinguishing features, fans, and detractors, all of which contribute to some rationale for why that language would be worthwhile to learn. In JavaScript's case, the language is worth learning for these reasons:

- Virtually any computing device today runs JavaScript "out of the box," thanks to the ubiquity of web browsers. No installation, download, nor setup is necessary.
- JavaScript programs integrate with web page content better than programs written in any other current programming language, enabling draggable objects, scrollable maps, animated and real-time effects, 3D rendering, and more, in "pure" web pages without plug-ins or extensions.

Regardless of people's misunderstandings about the language [Cro01], JavaScript is an extremely powerful [Cro08a] and extremely popular programming language (with some arguing that it is the *most* popular language in use today [Cro08b]). In the realm of programming languages, popularity frequently leads to importance [Sco05].

1.2   Writing and Running JavaScript

To write and run JavaScript programs, you'll need the following resources:

- A web browser

That's it. While technically this single requirement may be subject to a variety of qualifying statements (e.g., it has to be a "modern" web browser; JavaScript must be enabled; you must have a "good implementation" of JavaScript), in this book we take the optimistic (yet likely) stance that the web browser you use today is ready and willing to run JavaScript without any showstoppers. So fire up that browser and start with the simplest way to write and run JavaScript: your browser's own address field.

1.2.1   JavaScript URLs

Type this "address" into your web browser:

```
javascript:alert("Hello world!");
```

Make your browser go to this address (typically by pressing the *Enter* or *Return* key), and your browser should respond with a window that says, surprisingly enough, "Hello world!"

Figure 1.1 illustrates how this program looks in two browsers running on different operating systems (other browsers and platforms will look very similar). The underlying website doesn't affect the display—you've asked that the browser execute a JavaScript program (`alert("Hello world!");`) and the browser has obliged. To emphasize the ubiquity of web browsers and, by extension, JavaScript, screenshots throughout this book will intentionally mix browsers and platforms. Unless otherwise noted, everything in this book should run just fine on what you have. The final displays may look different, but the underlying behavior remains the same.

1.2.2   JavaScript Scratch Pages

Writing JavaScript in a one-line text field gets very old very quickly, so we've developed a "scratch page" through which you can enter longer scripts more easily. The website `http://javascript.cs.lmu.edu/scratch` hosts a rudimentary version of such a scratch page (Figure 1.2).

Figure 1.1 JavaScript "Hello world!" in Firefox on Linux and Chrome on Windows XP

Figure 1.2   A rudimentary JavaScript scratch page

To use this page, type a script into the text area and then click the *Run* button. For the trivial example from Section 1.2.1, you would type:

```
alert("Hello world!");
```

This is identical to what you typed into the browser's address field *except* for the `javascript:` prefix. That prefix was not part of the language; it was a marker that told the browser how the address text was to be interpreted. Because the scratch page expects and will only work properly with JavaScript, this prefix is now unnecessary.

Not surprisingly, clicking *Run* results in exactly the same behavior as before. This is because the browser is running exactly the same program—the only difference lies in *how* you entered this program into the web browser.

You might want to acclimate yourself to this environment a little bit by typing and running the short examples that follow using our rudimentary JavaScript scratch page. We'll leave them mostly unexplained for now; their purpose isn't to teach you the language yet, but rather to get you used to the process of typing in and running JavaScript code. If you have some programming experience under your belt already, these examples were chosen to preview some of JavaScript's interesting and unique aspects, so giving them a quick scan would still be useful.

Remember to type things exactly as shown. If the program doesn't behave as described, review what you typed to make sure that it matches the program given here. In addition, feel free to experiment with these scripts by making small changes and observing the results.

- This program simulates a single dice roll—every time you run it, you'll get a random number from one to six:

```
alert("You rolled a " +
    (Math.floor(Math.random() * 6) + 1) + "!");
```

- This program plays a baby game of "mad libs" based on a popular 1940s show tune:

```
alert("I like " +
    prompt("Please enter a city:") + " in " +
    prompt("Please enter a month:") + ", how about you?");
```

- This two-liner is great if you're lazy about capitalization:

```
alert(prompt("Enter something to shout:").toUpperCase());
alert(prompt('"Shout" something (all caps):').toLowerCase());
```

- Here's a script that runs another script entered by the user. Which do you think is more intriguing—the fact that this is possible in Java-Script, or the fact that such a script can be this short?

```
(new Function(prompt("Type in a script:")))();
```

Pay close attention to those parentheses—they have to be typed in *exactly* as shown. What do you think happens when the script that you type into this program's prompt is the program itself?

1.2.3 JavaScript Files

JavaScript URLs and scratch pages make it easy to write and experiment with JavaScript code quickly and conveniently. However, they do not handle the *distribution* and *sharing* of JavaScript programs once the code has been deemed ready for prime time.

To allow other users to partake of your latest and greatest scripts, you must save JavaScript programs in their own *files*. Web browsers can then download these files and run them, in much the same way that they run JavaScript URLs or the content of a JavaScript scratch page. The difference is that, instead of requiring direct typing (as you did with URLs and the scratch page), the web browsers can grab the code on their own.

Because this book strives to focus specifically on JavaScript as a programming language, and not JavaScript as a web technology, we'll purposely delay further coverage of the distribution and sharing of JavaScript code, especially for use in web browser applications, until Section 5.2.4.

1.2.4 Comments

Take a look at the following script. Notice anything unusual about it? (Needless to say, try typing it in and running it, too.)

```javascript
/*
 * We'll be echoing some text more than once.
 */
var echo = function(s) {
    return s + " " + s;
};

alert(echo("pizza"));
alert(echo("money"));

// We can also echo something given by the user.
alert(echo(prompt("Type something to echo:")));
```

The block between /* and */ at the beginning of the example, as well as the line starting with // near the end, don't look like code—they appear to be plain English. That's because they *are* plain English; text placed in between /* and */, as well as any text after two slashes (//) to the end of the line, are called *comments*. Comments allow human-speak to become part of a script, helping readers to understand the programmer's intent a little better. When JavaScript sees a /*, it knows to skip over everything after that until it sees */. When JavaScript sees //, it ignores everything from there to the end of the line.

The liberal inclusion of comments in code is highly encouraged in practice; no matter how great an expert one becomes with programming, it's often easier to read about something in plain English (or in any other language that you can speak, read, or write) than in code. This becomes especially compelling when you are part of a team of programmers and are reading code that you *didn't* write, or even when you are revisiting code that you've written but haven't seen for some time.

1.3 Your First Nontrivial Script

Now that we have established some straightforward mechanisms for writing and running JavaScript, let's take a look at a slightly more complex script. The purpose here is to show what a nontrivial script looks like; it is not necessary at this point that you understand the meaning of every line. Type the following into `http://javascript.cs.lmu.edu/scratch`:

```
// Ask the user for a phone number phrase.
var phrase = prompt('Please enter a phone number "phrase:"');

// Association of each letter with the number of the phone key.
var conversion =  A: 2, B: 2, C: 2, D: 3, E: 3, F: 3, G: 4,
    H: 4, I: 4, J: 5, K: 5, L: 5, M: 6, N: 6, O: 6, P: 7, Q: 7,
    R: 7, S: 7, T: 8, U: 8, V: 8, W: 9, X: 9, Y: 9, Z: 9 ;

// Build up the phone number one digit at a time.
var phoneNumber = "";
for (var index = 0; index < phrase.length; index += 1)
    var symbol = phrase[index].toUpperCase();
    phoneNumber += conversion[symbol] || symbol;


alert("You want to dial " + phoneNumber + ".");
```

As mentioned previously, type the code with absolute precision—copy everything *exactly* as shown. If you don't trust your own typing, you can visit `http://javascript.cs.lmu.edu/scratch/phrase-to-phone` for a version of the scratch page that has this script already "preloaded."

Assuming that you've typed this script correctly, clicking *Run* on the scratch page should display a dialog box that requests *Please enter a phone number "phrase:"*. Typing a valid phone number phrase such as (800) DENTIST or (310) GROCERY should then yield a second dialog box that gives the phone number equivalent of that phrase. Figure 1.3 shows the screenshot sequence based on the phone number (212) GET-CRTR.

Going over this script line by line, it is possible to see, even without prior programming experience, how much of its content corresponds to its behavior when run. First, remember that JavaScript ignores comments, because those items are meant for the humans who are reading the script.

Figure 1.3 Screenshots from your first nontrivial script, with (212) GET-CRTR as the phone number phrase to dial

The first line that is actually performed, then, is the one starting with `var phrase = prompt`...

When running in a web browser, JavaScript can perform `prompt`, which in this case makes the web browser display a dialog that asks for the "phone number phrase" to be dialed. Technically, `prompt` is called a "function"—you'll learn more about functions in Chapter 3.

To convert the letters in the phone number phrase into the digits 0–9, a *JavaScript object* named `conversion` is used. JavaScript objects are covered in greater detail in Chapter 4; for now, suffice it to say that `conversion` defines a list of possible letter-to-number "translations." Each translation (e.g., "A" corresponds to 2, "Q" corresponds to 7) is separated by a comma (`,`), with the letter and number parts separated by a colon (`:`). Letters appear before the colon, and the number that corresponds to each letter appears after the colon. For example, the letters "D," "E," and "F" all correspond to the number 3; "T," "U," and "V" correspond to the number 8; and so on.

By executing the block of code that starts with `for`, the script runs through each symbol in the phone number phrase, determining the digit that corresponds to the uppercase version of the symbol. Symbols that are not listed in `conversion` remain unconverted.

The `for` code block is called a *loop* because it repeats some activity according to certain conditions. In this case, the conversion sequence (the section in between the braces `{ }`) is repeated for every letter or symbol in the user-entered phone number phrase. Loops are discussed in greater detail in Section 2.4.4.

Once every symbol in the phrase has been processed, `alert` displays the result to the user—and we're done! The script then returns you to your regularly scheduled web page.

1.4   One More Nontrivial Script*

Here's another (optional) script to try out before we move on to look at
JavaScript in detail. As with the previous script, the purpose of this example is simply to acquaint you with the look and feel of a longer JavaScript
program, not to teach any aspect of the language. The script is available online if you're typing averse, at `http://javascript.cs.lmu.edu/scratch/`
`phone-to-phrase`:

```
/*
 * This function converts a digit into a random phone keypad letter
 * corresponding to that digit.  Non digits are not converted.
 */
var getRandomLetterFromDigit = function(digit) {
    var conversion = [ "ABC", "DEF", "GHI", "JKL", "MNO", "PQRS",
        "TUV", "WXYZ" ];

    // 0 and 1 don't convert into letters.
    var possibleLetters = conversion[digit - 2];
    return possibleLetters ?
      possibleLetters[Math.floor(possibleLetters.length * Math.random())] :
      digit;
};

// Ask the user for a phone number.
var phoneNumber = prompt("Please enter a phone number:");

/*
 * A "phone number" is any sequence of digits, spaces, parentheses,
 * and dashes.  The code right after "match" may look scary, but
 * is common in advanced scripts.  For now, just make sure to type
 * it in exactly.
 */
if (phoneNumber.match(/^[0-9\-\(\)\s]+$/)) {
    // Build the converted phone number, one character at a time.
    var mnemonic = "";
    for (var index = 0; index < phoneNumber.length; index += 1) {
        mnemonic += getRandomLetterFromDigit(phoneNumber[index]);
    }

    alert(mnemonic + " is a possible letter equivalent of " +
        phoneNumber + ".");

} else {
    // There was at least one character that was not a digit, space,
    // parenthesis, or dash.
    alert(phoneNumber + " cannot be interpreted as a phone number.");
}
```

When you run the script, you are first greeted by a request that you
enter a phone number. Typing a valid phone number (the script is actually quite lenient with what it considers to be a "phone number") yields
an `alert` that gives a randomly chosen letter equivalent to that number.
Figure 1.4 shows screenshots based on the phone number 555-1212.

Don't worry if the output in the figure isn't the same as what you see
on your own screen—remember that each of the digits 2–9 on a telephone

Figure 1.4 Screenshots from your second nontrivial script, with 555-1212 as the phone number to convert

corresponds to several possible letters, and this letter is chosen at random by the script. What matters is that if you "dial" the randomly chosen phone number phrase, you'll end up dialing the phone number that was entered (555-1212 in Figure 1.4).

This script involves functions (Chapter 3), objects (Chapter 4), and loops (Section 2.4.4), plus a few more features of the JavaScript language—some basic, some advanced. For now, we'll leave it at that. Feel free to play with or modify this script before moving on.

This example completes our initial look at the JavaScript language; in the interest of getting you to try things out and see some results right away, we have taken the approach of starting with examples but skipping some details. The remaining chapters delve deeper into the language itself, and the book concludes with an overview of how JavaScript and its features are used to create interactive web-based applications.

Chapter Summary

- JavaScript is the world's most popular programming language. Almost every computer with a web browser (including some cell phones and embedded devices) will run it "out of the box."

- To start programming in JavaScript, all you need is just a web browser.

- JavaScript can be executed by typing one-line `javascript:` URLs into a browser, or by using a browser-based scratch page. The code, once finalized, can then be stored, distributed, and shared using files.

- Scripts contain both code, representing things for the computer to do, and comments, representing information meant for the human readers of these scripts.

- The `prompt` and `alert` functions, which are built into web browsers running JavaScript, are, respectively, the simplest ways to request information from (*input*) and display information to (*output*) the script's user.

Exercises

1. Run the following program (1) as a one-line JavaScript URL and (2) as text entered into a scratch page or console.

```
alert("Hello, " + prompt("What's your name?"));
```

2. Try to run each of the sample programs given in Section 1.2.2 using the JavaScript URL approach instead of a scratch page.

(a) Is it possible to do this?

(b) What does the answer to part (a) tell you about how JavaScript handles spacing and new or blank lines?

3. Run the following one-line scripts (remember to type them in *exactly* as shown!) and note what appears. Explain the relationships between what was in the **alert** parentheses and what was displayed.

(a) alert("Good night and good" + "luck.");

(b) alert(2 + 10);

(c) alert(5 > 9);

(d) alert(/* Do the right thing. */);

(e) alert(Math.sqrt(-1));

4. The following one-line script (remember to type it in *exactly* as shown!) asks for some input from you and displays something back:

```
alert(prompt("Type something:"));
```

(a) Run the script and type 2 + 10 as input. What is displayed?

(b) Run the script and type 5 > 9 as input. What is displayed?

(c) Run the script and type Math.sqrt(-1) as input. What is displayed?

(d) Run the script and click the *Cancel* button. What is displayed?

(e) Briefly, and in your own words, describe what the script does.

5. Look up the range of values within which JavaScript's Math.random function returns its results. Also look up what Math.floor does. Can you write a general "formula" for generating random numbers greater than or equal to *a* but less than *b*? What if you want random *integers*?

6. Type and run this script, which includes a block comment inside another block comment:

```
/* A comment /* inside */ a comment. */
alert("Done!");
```

What happens (or doesn't happen)? Hazard a guess as to why Java-Script behaved in this manner.

7. Type and run this script, which uses the + operator to combine two expressions:

```
alert(1 + 1);
alert("1" + "1");
```

What is displayed? Hazard a guess as to why JavaScript behaved in this manner.

8. The following script is a variation on the one in Exercise 7; this time, the user gets to choose what is +-ed together:

```
alert(prompt("First thing to add: ") + prompt("Second thing to add: "));
```

Type and run this script. Enter 1 and 1 as input, as well as other combinations. What is displayed? Does this confirm or contradict your guess as to what + does?

9. Older phones, particularly those with rotary dials, did not include the letters Q and Z as possible conversions for the numbers 7 and 9, respectively. Modify the script on page 6 so that it is "backward compatible" with these older phones.

Basic JavaScript

Now that you have had a chance to run some simple JavaScript programs, we're ready for a technical look at the basic elements of the language itself.

2.1 Expressions

We'll start our overview of the language with expressions. An *expression* is code that is *evaluated*. Let's evaluate some expressions:

```
2               ⇒ 2
2 + 8.1 * 5     ⇒ 42.5
(2 + 8.1) * 5   ⇒ 50.5
9 > 4           ⇒ true
"dog" + "house" ⇒ "doghouse"
```

Expressions are made up of *values*, such as `8.1`, `true`, and `"dog"`, and *operators*, such as `+` (addition) and `*` (multiplication). Every value in JavaScript is either

- A *Boolean* (`true` or `false`),
- A number,
- A string,
- The special value `undefined`,
- The special value `null`, or
- An object.

We'll discuss Booleans, numbers, and strings first. We'll cover `undefined` in Section 2.3, and objects and `null` in Chapter 4.

2.1.1 Booleans

The Boolean values `true` and `false` are most often seen as the results of *comparisons*—expressions that compute whether two values are equal (`===`), not equal (`!==`), or ordered in some fashion (`<`, `<=`, `>=`, or `>`).

$$7 === 5 \Rightarrow \text{false} \quad \text{(equal to)}$$
$$8 !== 3 \Rightarrow \text{true} \quad \text{(not equal to)}$$
$$12 <= 12 \Rightarrow \text{true} \quad \text{(less than or equal to)}$$

JavaScript provides operators on Boolean values, including these:

- `&&` ("and"): `x && y` is true if and only if `x` and `y` are both true.
- `||` ("or"): `x || y` is true if and only if either `x` or `y`, or both, are true.
- `^` ("exclusive or"): `x ^ y` is true if and only if exactly one of `x` and `y` is true (not both).
- `!` ("not"): `!x` is true if and only if `x` is false.

The following table summarizes these relationships:

x	y	x && y	x || y	x ^ y	!x
true	true	true	true	false	false
true	false	false	true	true	false
false	true	false	true	true	true
false	false	false	false	false	true

Do not confuse the operators `&&` and `||` with `&` and `|`; the latter two are little-used in JavaScript applications. Also, do not confuse the `===` and `!==` operators with their cousins `==` and `!=` [Cro08a, p. 109]. The `==` operator, for example, considers a few things to be equal to each other that you might not expect; however, experienced programmers sometimes find them useful.

2.1.2 Numbers

You write numbers pretty much as you'd expect: `1729`, `3.141592`, and `299792458`. The letter `E` (or `e`) sandwiched between two numbers expresses the value "the number before E times 10 raised to the number after E" (also known as scientific notation):

$$3.6288E6 \Rightarrow 3.6288 \times 10^6 \Rightarrow 3628800$$
$$5.390E-44 \Rightarrow 5.390 \times 10^{-44}$$
$$4.63e170 \Rightarrow 4.63 \times 10^{170}$$

Operators on numbers include + (addition), - (subtraction), * (multiplication), / (division), and % (modulo). The modulo operator computes the remainder after division:

$$18 \text{ \% } 5 \Rightarrow 3$$
$$31.5 \text{ \% } 2.125 \Rightarrow 1.75$$

Other operations include `Math.floor(x)`, which produces the largest whole number less than or equal to x; `Math.ceil(x)`, which produces the smallest whole number greater than or equal to x; `Math.sqrt(x)`, which produces $\sqrt{x}$; `Math.pow(x, y)`, which produces x^y; and `Math.random()`, which produces a random number between 0 and 1.

```
Math.floor(2.8)   ⇒ 2
Math.floor(-2.8)  ⇒ -3
Math.ceil(2.8)    ⇒ 3
Math.ceil(-5)     ⇒ -5
Math.sqrt(100)    ⇒ 10
Math.pow(2.5, 4)  ⇒ 39.0625
```

In JavaScript, as in most programming languages, numbers are assumed to be stored in finite storage locations in a computer's memory, so there are limits to the set of numbers that can be represented. There is a largest finite number (JavaScript's is approximately 1.79×10^{308})[1] and a smallest finite number (approximately -1.79×10^{308}). Any computation producing a value larger than the largest finite number (or smaller than the smallest) yields the special value `Infinity` (or `-Infinity`).

```
2E200 * 73.987E150 ⇒ Infinity
-1e309             ⇒ -Infinity
```

Having numbers digitally represented limits not only the *size* of numbers, but also their *precision*. This may cause some surprises:

```
12157692622039623539       ⇒ 12157692622039624000
12157692622039623539 + 1 ⇒ 12157692622039624000
1e200 === 1e200 + 1        ⇒ true
4.18e − 1000               ⇒ 0
0.1 + 0.2                  ⇒ 0.30000000000000004
0.3 === 0.1 + 0.2          ⇒ false
```

---

1. Or $2^{1024} - 2^{972}$ to be exact.

In practice, you usually won't run into these cases, but it is important to be aware they exist! Here are some tips to help you cope:

- The representable numbers are packed most tightly around zero; in fact, more than half of them are between -1 and 1. The farther you stray from 0, the more spread out they become.

- All integers (the technical term for "whole number") between the values -9007199254740992 and 9007199254740992 are represented exactly. Unless you're doing financial calculations in excessively devalued currencies, you can count without worry.

- Computations involving (or yielding) large integers or non-integers will often produce nonexact results.

The special value NaN, meaning *Not a Number*, pops up whenever a computation produces something that is, well, not a number.

$$0 \; / \; 0 \qquad\qquad \Rightarrow \texttt{NaN}$$
$$\texttt{"dog" - "cat"} \qquad \Rightarrow \texttt{NaN}$$
$$\texttt{Infinity - Infinity} \Rightarrow \texttt{NaN}$$
$$\texttt{NaN + 16} \qquad\qquad \Rightarrow \texttt{NaN}$$
$$\texttt{NaN === NaN} \qquad \Rightarrow \texttt{false}$$

The last example is somewhat surprising: NaN isn't equal to anything, not even NaN! To determine whether something is not a number, use **isNaN**:

$$\texttt{isNaN(2.718281828)} \Rightarrow \texttt{false}$$
$$\texttt{isNaN(NaN)} \qquad\;\; \Rightarrow \texttt{true}$$
$$\texttt{isNaN("water")} \quad\; \Rightarrow \texttt{true}$$
$$\texttt{isNaN(Infinity)} \;\; \Rightarrow \texttt{false}$$

2.1.3 Strings

A *string* is a sequence of characters from the Unicode [Uni06] character set. Each character has a unique number called its *codepoint*. By convention, codepoints are written in hex.[2] Here are some examples:

F1	LATIN SMALL LETTER N WITH TILDE
03B8	GREEK SMALL LETTER THETA
095A	DEVANAGARI LETTER GHHA

---

2. Hex, or hexadecimal, numerals are base 16; they're ordered like this: 0, 1, 2, 3, 4, 5, 6, 7, 8, 9, a, b, c, d, e, f, 10, 11, 12, ... , 1f, 20, ... , 9e, 9f, a0, a1, ... , ff, 100, ...

11F4	HANGUL JONGSEONG KAPYEOUNPHIEUPH
13C9	CHEROKEE LETTER QUO
265B	BLACK CHESS QUEEN
2678	RECYCLING SYMBOL FOR TYPE-6 PLASTICS
FE7C	ARABIC SHADDA ISOLATED FORM
1D122	MUSICAL SYMBOL F CLEF

An online version of the codepoint-to-character mapping can be found in the source [Uni08].

String values are written within double quotes (e.g., `"hello"`) or single quotes (e.g., `'hello'`), and *must fit on one line*. The backslash character "\" is special; it combines with subsequent characters to express characters we may not be able to type, among other things. Backslash combinations are called *escape sequences*, several of which are given in Table 2.1.

Here are two examples of strings:

- `'I\xf1es said, "It\'s me."'` This 20-character string (about Inés) illustrates the need for escaping a quote character.
- `"\u0386\u03b8\u03b7\u03bd\u03b1"` This string names the capital of Greece, $A\theta\eta\nu\alpha$.

The "control characters" mentioned in Table 2.1 affect the way a string is displayed. The most common of these are the newline `\n`, which causes the rest of the string to be written on the next line, and the tab, `\t`, which

`\'`	The single-quote character (used to get the single-quote character in a string surrounded by single quotes)
`\"`	The double-quote character (used to get the double-quote character in a string surrounded by double quotes)
`\x`*hh*	Where *hh* is a two-digit hexadecimal value, is the character whose codepoint is that value
`\u`*hhhh*	Where *hhhh* is a four-digit hexadecimal value, is the character whose codepoint is that value
`\n, \t, \b,` `\f, \r, \v`	The *control* characters newline, tab, backspace, formfeed, carriage return, and vertical tab
`\\`	The backslash character itself

Table 2.1 JavaScript escape sequences

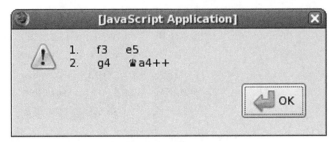

Figure 2.1   A string with tabs and newlines

can be used to align text in columns. Here's a fun one-line script that alerts
a string with tabs and newlines; Figure 2.1 shows the output.

```
alert("1.\tf3\te5\n2.\tg4\t\u265ba4++");
```

JavaScript provides dozens of string operations, such as finding the
string's length (number of characters), translations to uppercase and low-
ercase, and replacing parts of the string.

```
"Hello, there".length               ⇒ 12
"Hello, there".toLowerCase()         ⇒ "hello, there"
"Hello, there".toUpperCase()         ⇒ "HELLO, THERE"
"Hello, there".replace("ello", "i")  ⇒ "Hi, there"
```

Sometimes you'd like to know where in a string a certain character can
be found, or find out which character is at a given position. In JavaScript,
the first character in a string is at *index* 0, the second at index 1, the third
at index 2, and so on. The character at position p within string s is found
with the expression s.charAt(p). Text within a string can be located with
indexOf and lastIndexOf. The expression s.substring(x,y) produces a
string consisting of all characters of string s from index x up to but *not
including* the character at index y.

```
"Some text".charAt(7)        ⇒ "x"
"Some text".indexOf("me")    ⇒ 2
"Some text".lastIndexOf("e") ⇒ 6
"Some text".substring(3, 7)  ⇒ "e te"
```

2.1.4 Type Conversion

JavaScript operators expect operands of certain types; for example, ∗ mul-
tiplies numbers, toUpperCase() capitalizes strings, and so on. However,

when an operator is applied to a value of an unexpected type, JavaScript will find a suitable treatment for your value. When a Boolean is expected, 0, `false`, the empty string (`""` or `''`), `undefined`, `null`, and NaN are treated as false and everything else is treated as true. When a string is expected, nonstrings are treated as you might expect—for example, `true` as `"true"` and 100 as `"100"`.[3] When a number is expected, `undefined` is treated as NaN, `null` and `false` are 0, and `true` is 1. Strings that look like numbers are treated as numbers; those that don't are treated like NaN. String-to-number conversion kicks in for most arithmetic operations, but not for addition, because that pesky plus symbol (+) does string concatenation instead!

$$
\begin{array}{ll}
\texttt{"dog" + 256} & \Rightarrow \texttt{"dog256"} \\
\texttt{"dog" * 256} & \Rightarrow \texttt{NaN} \\
\texttt{"100" + 256} & \Rightarrow \texttt{100256} \\
\texttt{"100" * 256} & \Rightarrow \texttt{25600} \\
\texttt{"100" * "256"} & \Rightarrow \texttt{25600}
\end{array}
$$

2.2 Variables

Values can be stored in *variables* for later use. You must first *declare* a variable to bring it into existence. You may specify an initial value in the declaration; if you do not, the value stored in the variable will be the special value `undefined`.

After the declaration, you are free to use the variable. You can also store a new value in a variable by a process called *assignment*, which *replaces (overwrites) the existing value stored in the variable.*

```
var x = 2;         // Declares x, initializing it to 2.
alert(x);          // Alerts 2.
alert(10 * x);     // Alerts 20.
var y;             // Declares y, without an explicit initial value.
alert(y);          // Alerts undefined.
y = x * 5;         // Assigns 10 to y, because x is still 2.
var z = y;         // Declares z, initializes it to 10.
y = "dog";         // Assigns "dog" to y, overwriting the old value 10.
alert(y + z);      // Alerts "dog10", because z is still 10.
```

---

3. We'll see how objects are treated as strings in Chapter 4.

Interestingly, = is not the only assignment operator:

```
var x = 5;
x += 30;        // Same as x = x + 30, x now 35.
x -= 2;         // Same as x = x - 2, x now 33.
x *= -4;        // Same as x = x * -4, x now -132.
x = false;
x ||= true;     // Same as x = x || true, x now true.
```

Variables can also be updated with the ++ (increment) and −− (decrement) operators. These can be tricky![4] When placed in front of a variable, the operator updates the variable *before* the expression is evaluated. If the operator follows the variable, the variable is updated *after* the evaluation.

```
var x = 5;
x++;            // Now x is 6.
var y = x++;    // y gets 6, THEN x becomes 7.
var z = ++x;    // First x is bumped to 8, THEN z gets 8.
```

Attempting to *use* a variable without first declaring it generates an error, as the following script illustrates:

```
alert(next_song);
```

The actual error notification you'll receive depends on what you're using to run JavaScript; perhaps a window will pop up with the words "next_song is not defined." Some systems have a *console*, *error*, or *debug* window that maintains a running list of issues.

Perhaps strangely, this script gives no such error:

```
next_song = "Purple Haze";
```

We say "strange" because this line doesn't look like a declaration; it looks like an assignment. JavaScript, though, treats it as a declaration if the variable isn't already declared. This automatic declaration is now considered by many experts to be a language design flaw, for technical reasons beyond the scope of this book. Its existence means it is important to *always use* var *when declaring variables.*

Variable names are subject to two rules. First, the name must begin with a letter, the $ character, or the _ character, and contain only letters, digits, _'s, and $'s thereafter.

---

4. They are also unnecessary, with good reasons to avoid them completely. See [Cro08a, p. 112] for details.

Second, you cannot use any of JavaScript's *reserved words*: abstract, boolean, break, byte, case, catch, char, class, const, continue, debugger, default, delete, do, double, else, enum, export, extends, final, finally, float, for, function, goto, if, implements, import, in, instanceof, int, interface, long, native, new, package, private, protected, public, return, short, static, super, switch, synchronized, this, throw, throws, transient, try, typeof, var, void, volatile, while, with. JavaScript reserves these words for possible special meanings; we've seen, for example, how var introduces variable declarations.

2.3 Arrays

An *array* is composed of a sequence of values. You identify the first value in array a as a[0], the second as a[1], and so on. Arrays are written with square brackets (e.g., [2, 3, 7]). You can add items to the end of the array with push and to the beginning of the array with unshift. You can remove items from the end with pop and from the front with shift. You can also sort arrays.

```
var a = [];           // a is an array of length 0.
var b = [3, 5];       // b has length 2.
b.push(2);            // Now b is [3, 5, 2].
b.unshift(7);         // Now b is [7, 3, 5, 2].
a.push(3, 10, 5);     // Now a is [3, 10, 5].
alert(a.pop());       // Alerts 5 and changes a to [3, 10].
alert(a.shift());     // Alerts 3 and changes a to [10].
b.push(a[0], 1);      // b is now [7, 3, 5, 2, 10, 1].
b.sort();             // b is now [1, 10, 2, 3, 5, 7].
```

What? How did 10 get between 1 and 2? The answer is that because arrays can contain any kind of value—not just numbers—JavaScript treats all values as strings when sorting. Also, the string "1" is less than "10", which is less than "2". So how do you sort numerically? You'll have to wait until the next chapter for the answer to this question.

Given an array a, the expression a.length yields the number of elements in a. Assigning to a.length may grow or shrink the array; new values are set to undefined. You may also grow an array by assigning to an index position beyond the end of the array.

```
var a = [9, 3, 2, 1, 8, 7, 3];
a[20] = 6;            // a[7] through a[19] now undefined.
alert(a.length);      // Alerts 21.
a.length = 50;        // a[21] through a[49] all undefined.
a.length = 3;         // a is now [9, 3, 2].
```

2.4   Statements

We round out our overview of basic JavaScript by looking at *statements*. Whereas expressions compute values, statements produce actions. A script is, in fact, a *sequence of statements*, each of which is *executed* when the script is run.

In this section we cover the most common JavaScript statements, providing example scripts that contain them. You will notice that we finish every statement with a semicolon (;), unless it already ends with a right curly brace (}). While not strictly required, this is a *highly* recommended practice. Leaving out semicolons can be very problematic (see [ECM99, Sec. 7.9]).

2.4.1   The Declaration Statement

A *declaration statement* just declares a variable.

```
var count = 0;
var dogs = ["Sparky", "Spot", "Spike"];
var response;
```

2.4.2   The Expression Statement

An *expression statement* evaluates an expression and ignores its value. Therefore the only useful kinds of expression statements are those that have an effect on subsequent computation, like assignment.

```
2 + 2;              // A legal statement, but completely useless.
x = 1 + (y = 4);    // Assigns 4 to y and then 5 to x.
count++;            // Incrementing is actually quite common.
alert("hi");        // This one definitely has a visible effect.
```

2.4.3   Conditional Execution

Programs often need to do one thing under certain conditions and something else under other conditions. The `if` statement does exactly one of a number of alternative executions, based on various conditions. The general form of this statement is to have one `if` part, zero or more `else if` parts, and an optional `else` part. The conditions are evaluated in order, from top to bottom.

```
if (score >= 90) {
    grade = "A";
} else if (score >= 80) {
    grade = "B";
```

```
} else if (score >= 70) {
    grade = "C";
} else {
    grade = "F";
}
alert(score + " is a " + grade);
```

Sometimes you may prefer a *conditional expression* in place of an `if` statement: x ? y : z evaluates to y if x evaluates to `true` and z otherwise. For example, instead of

```
if (latitude >= 0) {
    hemisphere = "north";
} else {
    hemisphere = "south";
}
```

you can write

```
hemisphere = (latitude >= 0) ? "north" : "south";
```

Another kind of conditional statement, the `switch` statement, compares a value against a sequence of *cases*, until it finds one that is equal to (`===`) the value, and begins executing statements at that point. An optional `default` case will match any value at all.

```
switch (direction.toLowerCase()) {
    case "north": row -= 1; break;
    case "south": row += 1; break;
    case "east": column += 1; break;
    case "west": column -= 1; break;
    default: alert("Illegal direction");
}
```

A `break` statement will terminate the entire `switch` statement. It's considered good practice to finish each case with a `break`;[5] otherwise, execution will "fall through" to the next case.

2.4.4 Loops

The term *loop* refers to code that is executed over and over again. JavaScript's `while` statement executes code repeatedly as long as a condition evaluates to true. The following example generates a random letter and

---

5. Or a `return` statement, which we will see in the next chapter.

asks a user to guess the letter. If the user's guess is not correct, the script records the number of guesses and repeats the prompt. Only when the guess is correct does the `while` statement finish, and the script notifies the user of the number of guesses.

```
// Get a random number between 0 and 25, inclusive.
var index = Math.floor(Math.random() * 26);

// Get a random letter.
var letter = "ABCDEFGHIJKLMNOPQRSTUVWXYZ".charAt(index);

var number_of_tries = 1;
while (prompt("Guess my letter") !== letter) {
    number_of_tries++;
}
alert("Guessed it in " + number_of_tries + " tries");
```

The second kind of loop, the `for` statement, also loops as long as a condition is true, but lets the programmer pack in some additional code into a small space. The general form of this statement is

$$\text{for } (init \; ; \; test \; ; \; each) \; \{ \; body \; \}$$

The *init* code is run first, then as long as *test* is true, runs the *body* followed by *each*. For example:

```
// Alerts even numbers from 4 through 20.
for (var number = 4; number <= 20; number += 2) {
    alert(number + " is even");
}
```

Here `number` is initialized to 4. Because this value is less than or equal to 20, the script alerts `"4 is even"` and then bumps `number` to 6. Because 6 is now less than or equal to 20, we next see `"6 is even"` and `number` becomes 8. The last value alerted is 20, because `number` will subsequently be bumped to 22 and the test condition will become `false`, ending the loop.

The use of `for` statements is very common when writing code that processes arrays. In the following example, we process the strings `words[0]`, `words[1]`, `words[2]`, and so on, by incrementing the variable `i` each time we pass through the loop.

```
// Alerts a string made up of the initial characters of each array item.
var words = ["Rats", "are", "very", "intellegent"];
var result = "";
for (var i = 0; i < words.length; i++) {
    result += words[i].charAt(0);
}
alert(result);
```

JavaScript also has another kind of `for` loop that we will encounter in Chapter 4.

The `break` statement will immediately terminate an entire loop (it "breaks out," in a way). This behavior is especially useful when you are looking for something in an array.

```javascript
// Find the index position of the first even number in array.
for (var i = 0; i < array.length; i++) {
    if (array[i] % 2 === 0) {
        alert("Even number found at position " + i);
        break;
    }
}
```

The `continue` statement immediately starts the next iteration of a loop, without finishing the current one. It is useful when some, but not all, of the iterations in your loop produce useful information.

```javascript
// Computes the sum of all positive values in array.
var sum = 0;
for (var i = 0; i < array.length; i++) {
    if (array[i] <= 0) {
        continue;                   // Skip nonpositives.
    }
    sum += array[i];                // Accumulate positives.
}
alert("Sum of positives is " + sum);
```

This completes our overview of the most basic elements of JavaScript. We've seen only a small part of the language, but you should now be able to write simple scripts on your own. Some of the exercises in this chapter encourage you to do so.

Chapter Summary

- Scripts are made up of statements, many of which evaluate expressions.
- Every JavaScript value is either **undefined**, **null**, a number, a Boolean, a string, or an object.
- JavaScript numbers have size and precision limits, so many computations return approximate results.
- We can store the results of evaluating expressions in variables and retrieve them later. Variables must be declared before being used. If an initial value is not given in the declaration, the variable's value is **undefined**.

- The expression x === y computes whether x and y are equal, while x = y assigns the value of y to x. The expression x == y is another kind of equality test, but should generally be avoided because its behavior, while completely specified in the official language definition, is often unexpected.
- An array is a collection of values, indexed from 0.
- JavaScript statements include declarations, expression statements, conditionals, loops, and break and continue statements.

Exercises

1. Let x = 10, y = 4, b = false. Evaluate the following expressions:

   (a) x * y > 25 && !b ? y % -3 : 22

   (b) --y * 4 === 2 || (b ^ true)

2. Find out about the following numeric operators: <<, >>, >>>, ~, &, |, and ^. Describe each of them in your own words. Experiment with them in a console or scratch page.

3. Consult a JavaScript reference manual (print or online) and make a list of all Math operations in the language.

4. What does the following expression represent?

```
Math.random() < 0.75 ? "Heads" : "Tails"
```

5. Evaluate the following expressions:

   (a) 5 / 0

   (b) 0 / 0

   (c) Infinity + Infinity

   (d) Infinity - Infinity

   (e) Infinity * Infinity

   (f) Infinity / Infinity

6. Explain, in your own words, the difference between a variable having the value undefined, and the error that occurs when a variable has not been defined.

7. Write a (one-line) script that alerts a greeting message in Armenian, Arabic, Hebrew, Hindi, Chinese, or any other language using a non-Latin script.

8. Look up the details of the array operations slice and splice on the Web or in a JavaScript reference book. Experiment with these

operations in a scratch page until you are able to explain them in your own words.

9. What is the expression x < y ? x : y good for?

10. In the "Rats are very intelligent" example on page 24, what happens when one of the array items is the empty string? What happens when an array item is a number? The value undefined? You will want to modify and run the script to find out.

11. Look up information on the string split operation. Evaluate the following expressions:

(a) "one two three".split(" ");

(b) "abracadabra".split("a");

12. Write a script that prompts the user for a string containing numbers separated by spaces, and then alerts the minimum value, the maximum value, and the sum. For example, if the input is 2 -9 3 4 1, then the script should alert Minimum is -9, Maximum is 4, Sum is 1.

13. Write a script that repeatedly prompts a user to enter a word or phrase, until the empty string is entered. Collect all of the inputs into an array while they are being input. Convert each of the strings to uppercase, and then sort the array. Finally, alert the array, showing each array entry on its own line.

14. Write a script that prompts the user for a string, then alerts whether the input string is a *palindrome*. A palindrome is a string that is spelled the same both forward and backward—for example, "I", "bob",
"racecar". Experiment with variations of the script that are insensitive to the case of letters (e.g., allowing "Abba" code) and that ignore nonletters (e.g., allowing "Madam, I'm Adam").

15. Explain, in your own words, the behavior of each of the following scripts:

```
var i = 0;
while (i < 10) {
    continue;
    i++;
}
alert("All done");
```

```
for (var i = 0; i < 10; i++) {
    continue;
}
alert("All done");
```

Functions

A *function* is an object that carries out a specific computation; it is written once but can be run over and over again. This chapter illustrates how to define and use functions, spending some time on one of JavaScript's most useful and powerful features: the ability to pass functions as arguments to other functions.

3.1 Function Definitions and Function Calls

Conceptually, a function transforms inputs to outputs. Figure 3.1 shows the "computation" of an account balance after t years, given a starting balance p, and an annual percentage rate r, compounded n times per year.

In JavaScript, a function consists of a block of executable code, called its *body*, together with zero or more "inputs," called *parameters*. The following three examples show how function values are written in JavaScript.

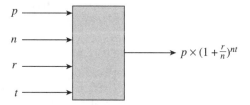

Figure 3.1 Function inputs and outputs

```
// A function that computes the cube of a number.
function(x) { return x * x * x; }

// A function that computes an account balance.
function(p, n, r, t) { return p * Math.pow(1 + (r / n), n * t); }

// A function that alerts a message twice, without returning anything.
function(message) { alert(message); alert("I said: " + message + "!"); }
```

Because functions exist to be used repeatedly, you will generally see function values assigned to variables.

```
// Returns the area of a circle with radius r.
var circle_area = function(r) { return Math.PI * r * r; };

// Returns the sum of all elements in an array.
var sum = function(a) {
    var result = 0;
    for (var i = 0; i < a.length; i++) {
        result += a[i];
    }
    return result;
};

// Reverses all strings in an array.
var reverse_all = function(a) {
    for (var i = 0; i < a.length; i++) {
        a[i] = a[i].reverse();
    }
};

// Uppercases all strings in an array.
var uppercase_all = function(a) {
    for (var i = 0; i < a.length; i++) {
        a[i] = a[i].toUpperCase();
    }
};

// Returns whether x evenly divides y.
var divides = function(x, y) { return y % x === 0; };
```

To use, or "call," a function, you "pass" it a parenthesized list of *arguments*. The function's body will be run with those arguments in place of its parameters. A `return` statement, if any, is used to pass the result of a computation back to the "caller." Functions that finish without executing a `return` statement return `undefined`.

```
// Assign a function value to a variable.
var cubed = function(x) { return x * x * x; };
```

```
// Call the function, using the return value.
var numberOfRubiksCubeBlocks = cubed(3) - 1;

// Function calls can be nested.
alert(cubed(5));                    // Alerts 125.
```

If you don't pass enough arguments, the extra parameters will be initialized to **undefined**.

```
var show = function(x, y) { alert(x + " " + y); }

show(1);                // Alerts "1 undefined".
```

It is not uncommon to see functions with *no* parameters. For example:

```
var diceRoll = function() { return 1 + Math.floor(6 * Math.random()); }
```

To run this function, you must write `diceRoll()`, not simply `diceRoll`. The former expression calls the function; the latter simply *is* the function. Figure 3.2 shows the difference.

```
alert(diceRoll() + "\n"
    + diceRoll() + "\n"
    + diceRoll() + "\n"
    + diceRoll
);
```

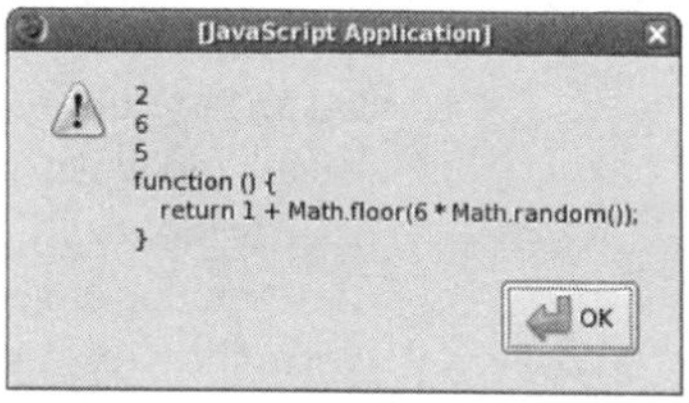

Figure 3.2 Function values versus function calls

3.2 Variable Scope

Each time you call a function, JavaScript immediately creates something called an *activation object* that holds all the parameters and any variables defined in the body of the function. It also creates and initializes a special variable called **arguments**, though this is beyond the scope of this book. These variables are *different* from variables outside of the function—even those with the same name, as we shall soon see.

We'll use the following script to illustrate how JavaScript treats variables and parameters:

```
/*  1 */ var remove_spaces = true;
/*  2 */ var message = prompt("Enter a message");
/*  3 */ var codepoints = function(text) {
/*  4 */     var message = [];
/*  5 */     for (var i = 0; i < text.length; i++) {
/*  6 */         if (remove_spaces && text[i] === " ") {
/*  7 */             continue;
/*  8 */         }
/*  9 */         message.push(text.charCodeAt(i));
/* 10 */     }
/* 11 */     return message;
/* 12 */ };
/* 13 */ alert(codepoints(message));
```

This script prompts the user for a message and then alerts the codepoints of each character in the message, except for the space characters. If the user enters Mbôlô, the script will alert 77, 98, 244, 108, 244.

The script defines three *top-level* variables (remove_spaces, message, and codepoints), where "top-level" is another way of saying "defined outside of any function." The function referred to by (top-level) variable codepoints has one parameter (text) and two *local* variables (message and i). Local variables are variables defined within some function.

The script begins execution on line 1, and declares a new variable called remove_spaces, initializing it to true. This new variable is added to the collection of preexisting top-level variables, including prompt, alert, Infinity, and dozens more. Next, on line 2, a new variable is declared and initialized with whatever the user types into the prompt box. For the sake of argument, let's say the user entered Bună dzua. On line 3, we declare yet another top-level variable, codepoints, whose initial value is a function. Note that executing line 3 *just declares* the variable codepoints; it does *not* call the function. This brings us to the situation in Figure 3.3.

Next we execute line 13, the first part of which is the actual call of function codepoints. JavaScript builds the activation object for this function and fills it with the parameters and local variables. Parameters will be immediately initialized with their corresponding arguments, but local variables are immediately initialized to undefined.[1] See Figure 3.4.

On line 4, we assign the empty array value [ ] to the *local* variable message. Note that there are *two* variables called message: one top-level

---

1. Note this very important distinction between top-level variables and local variables. Top-level variables are declared and initialized when they are first encountered, but local variables come into existence *immediately* when the function in which they are declared is called.

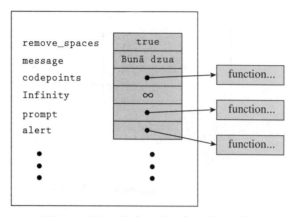

Figure 3.3 Before the function call

variable and one variable that is local to the `codepoints` function. Updating the local variable in no way affects the top-level one, even though they share the same name.

In lines 5–11, the array `message` grows with the codepoints of every character in the variable `text`, except that space characters are skipped if the variable `remove_spaces` is true. The interesting thing here is that `remove_spaces` is defined outside the function; however, it can be referred to by code inside the function body. This is a common scenario in many programming languages: "outer" variables are visible to "inner" regions of a script. It is also very useful: `alert` and `prompt` and friends exist at the top level, and we don't want them hidden from function bodies. Figure 3.5 illustrates our situation at the end of the function body.

More technically, function activation objects are linked together, from the inside out, forming what is called a *scope chain*. When using a name from code inside the `codepoints` function, JavaScript first looks for that

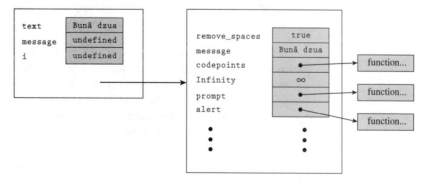

Figure 3.4 At function entry

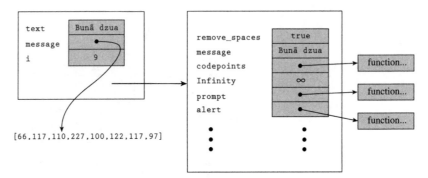

Figure 3.5   At the end of the function body

name in the function's activation object. If the name is not found, it moves along the scope chain and looks for the name in the next object. The object containing all the *top-level* variables is last on the chain. As a consequence:

- Inside the function, the name **message** will always refer to the inner variable of that name, never the outer one.

- Because the chain runs "outward" only, code outside of a function cannot see any variables inside the function.

The second point, though it follows directly from the language rules defining scope chains, still merits an example:

```
var say_hello = function() {
    var message = "Hello";
    alert(message + "!!!");
}

message = "Goodbye";    // This isn't the inner variable.
say_hello();            // Alerts "Hello!!!"
```

The fact that local variables are protected from outside interference means that functions are an excellent way to package and share code. Furthermore, a function gets its own copies of its local variables and parameters every time it is called, so you never have to worry about a variable named x defined in one function clashing with a variable named x defined in another function.[2] They are two separate variables.

---

2. The fact that each *call* gets its own copies supports an extremely powerful programming technique called *recursion*, whose underlying theory is explained in any computer science textbook.

3.3 Function Statements

JavaScript's function *statement* provides an alternative way to declare a variable and assign it a function value. The following statement declares and initializes a variable called `cubed`:

```
function cubed(x) {
    return x * x * x;
}
```

We prefer to use the longer form, as it makes clear that functions are values.

3.4 Functions as Arguments to Functions

All programmers realize at some point that writing the same code over and over is a bad thing. If you had to, say, encrypt a large batch of credit card numbers, you certainly wouldn't duplicate the 50 or so lines of encryption code for each credit card number. Rather, you would write an encryption function taking the credit card number as a parameter.[3] Now your code follows the DRY (Don't Repeat Yourself) principle—a good thing.

Sometimes code repetition is more subtle. Consider these two functions, both of which return arrays generated by manipulating each element of an input array in a particular way:

```
var square_all = function(a) {
    var result = [];
    for (var i = 0; i < a.length; i++) {
        result[i] = a[i] * a[i];
    }
    return result;
};

var capitalize_all = function(a) {
    var result = [];
    for (var i = 0; i < a.length; i++) {
        result[i] = a[i].toUpperCase();
    }
    return result;
};
```

These two functions *differ in only one small way.* The first function squares an element; the latter capitalizes it. Can we code the common

---

3. When this concept becomes second nature to you, you have moved beyond your programming white belt.

structure once and parametrize it by the small difference? JavaScript makes this *very* easy:

```
var do_all = function(a, f) {
    var result = [];
    for (var i = 0; i < a.length; i++) {
        result[i] = f(a[i]);
    }
    return result;
};
```

The actual operation you perform on each array element (e.g., squaring, capitalizing) is now passed as an argument:

```
var square_all = function(a) {
    return do_all(a, function(x) { return x * x; });
};

var capitalize_all = function(a) {
    return do_all(a, function(x) { return x.toUpperCase(); });
};
```

If placing an entire function value in the middle of a return statement looks cryptic, you can define these arguments separately:

```
var square = function(x) { return x * x; };
var capitalize = function(x) { return x.toUpperCase(); };

var square_all = function(a) { return do_all(a, square); };
var capitalize_all = function(a) { return do_all(a, capitalize}); };
```

Remember from the previous chapter how calling `a.sort()` sorted array `a` alphabetically? You can, if desired, pass a *comparison function* to `sort` to make it sort differently. A comparison function is a two-argument function returning a negative value if the first argument is less than the second, 0 if the two arguments are equal, and a positive value if the first argument is larger.

```
var a = [3, 6, 10, 1, 40, 25, 8, 73];
alert(a.sort());                              // Alphabetically.
alert(a.sort(function(x, y) { return x - y; })); // Numeric ascending.
alert(a.sort(function(x, y) { return y - x; })); // Numeric descending.
```

We've just shown that functions *can* be passed to other functions, but we haven't really said *why* this matters. We'll see in Chapter 5 that passing functions is JavaScript's way of handling user interaction in web pages. It also happens to be one of the most dominant programming paradigms in artificial intelligence programming. And, as described in [Spo06], it aids the construction of massively large, distributed applications.

3.5 Functions Returned from Functions*

Not only can functions be passed to other functions, but functions can be returned as well. Let's say you need a function that adds 10 to its argument, and another that adds 17. We can capture the similar parts of these functions in one place:

```
var incrementer = function(n) {
    return function(x) { return x + n; }
}

var add_ten = incrementer(10);
var add_seventeen = incrementer(17);
alert(add_ten(236));                    // Alerts 246.
```

The function add_ten and add_seventeen, as well as any value returned from calling incrementer, is called a *closure*. Closures play an integral role in some very sophisticated JavaScript structures, such as sequence generators and modules. These topics are well beyond the scope of this book, but details can be found in [Fla06] and [Cro08a].

Chapter Summary

- A function value is a parameterized block of code that can be run (or "called") as often as you wish.
- When calling a function, we pass arguments to its parameters. Excess parameters are initialized to undefined. Functions can return results to the caller via a return statement.
- JavaScript functions are values and, therefore, can be assigned to variables, passed as arguments to other functions, and returned from functions.

Exercises

1. Write a function that returns the average of its two arguments. For example, the call average(-2, 10) should return 4.

2. Write a function that returns the average of all items in an array. For example, `average([4, 5, 7, 2])` should return 4.5.

3. Write a function that returns the number of occurrences of a given character in a string. For example, given the string `"Rat-a-tat-tat"` and the character `t`, your function should return 5.

4. Explain, in detail, what is alerted by this script:

```
var x = 5;
var f = function() { alert(x); var x = 10; alert(x); };
f();
alert(x);
```

5. Explain, in detail, what happens when you run this script:

```
alert("Hello");
var alert = 2;
alert("World");
```

6. Write a function called `twice` that takes in a function f and a value x, and returns $f(f(x))$.

7. Define a function called `toTheEighthPower` that takes in a value x and returns x^8. Use the `square` function defined in this chapter and the `twice` function you defined in Exercise 6.

8. Suppose you tried to implement the `square_all` function we wrote in Section 3.4 using the incorrect expression `do_all(a, square())`. Explain why this is wrong.

9. Suppose you were asked by an employer, teacher, or friend to write a function that determines whether a given function would ever finish or whether it would run forever. In other words, you are asked to fill in the body of this function:

```
// Returns true if the call f() finishes; false if it runs forever.
var finishes = function(f) {
    // Fill this in...
}
```

Before attempting to implement this function, consider the following function:

```
var paradox = function() {
    if (finishes(paradox)) {
        while (true) { }
    }
};
```

Suppose function **paradox** finishes: The expression `finishes(paradox)` on line 2 will return true, but then it will run forever on line 3. Now suppose it doesn't finish: The call to `finishes` on line 2 will return false, at which point it will reach the end of its body and ... *finish*. Why does this mean that function `finishes` is logically, mathematically, scientifically *impossible* to write?

Objects

JavaScript values come in two flavors: simple values (numbers, Booleans, strings, null, and undefined) and *objects*. This chapter shows how to define and use objects.

4.1 Object Notation

In JavaScript, objects have *properties*, and properties have *values*. Property values may be objects as well, allowing complex structures to be defined. An *object literal* is an expression defining a new object; several examples follow.

```
var dress =
    { size: 4, color: "green", brand: "DKNY", price: 834.95 };

var location = {
    latitude: 31.131013,
    longitude: 29.976977
};

var song = {
    title: "This Town",
    track_number: 6,
    album: "Beauty and the Beat",
    artist: "The Go-Go's",
    authors: [ "Charlotte Caffey", "Jane Wiedlin" ],
    duration: 200
};
```

```
var p = {
    name: { first: "Ciarán", last: "O'Brien" },
    country: "Ireland",
    birth: { year: 1952, month: 2, day: 17 },
    kids: [ "Ciara", "Seán", "Bearach", "Máiréad", "Aisling" ]
};
```

After defining an object, you may access its properties with either a dot or square brackets.

$$p.country \qquad \Rightarrow \text{"Ireland"}$$
$$p["country"] \qquad \Rightarrow \text{"Ireland"}$$
$$p.birth.year \qquad \Rightarrow 1952$$
$$p.birth["year"] \qquad \Rightarrow 1952$$
$$p["birth"].year \qquad \Rightarrow 1952$$
$$p["birth"]["year"] \qquad \Rightarrow 1952$$
$$p.kids[1] \qquad \Rightarrow \text{"Seán"}$$
$$p["kids"][1] \qquad \Rightarrow \text{"Seán"}$$

Property names can be strings (with or without quotes) or non-negative integers (0, 1, 2, ...). Arrays, which we have seen before, are objects with integer properties and one called `length`. Functions are objects, too.

The dot notation for properties is a bit more concise, but cannot be used with integer properties (i.e., you can't say, `a.1`), nor can it be used if the property is a JavaScript reserved word (we saw these back on page 21). In these cases, the bracket notation is required (e.g., `a[10]`, `a["var"]`).

It's not necessary to fully specify all of the properties of an object when defining it. Instead, you can later add (or even delete) properties if you like:

```
var dog = {};                // An object with no properties.
dog.name = "Kärl";           // Now the object has one property.
alert(dog);
dog.breed = "Rottweiler";    // Now the object has two properties.
delete dog.name;             // Now one property again.
```

Object properties can be, and often are, function values. In such a function, the `this` expression refers to the object containing the function.

```
var vector = {
    i: 4,
    j: -3,
    magnitude: function() {return Math.sqrt(this.i*this.i+this.j*this.j);}
};
alert(vector.magnitude());        // Alerts 5
vector.i = 0;
alert(vector.magnitude());        // Alerts 3
```

4.2 Object Values

The following two facts about objects are essential to understanding how to use objects correctly and efficiently, and should be memorized:

1. Every evaluation of an object literal creates a brand-new object.

2. The *value* of an object literal expression is not really the object itself, but rather a *reference*, or *pointer*, to it.

We need to tell this story in pictures. Figure 4.1 shows the result of executing a script that declares three variables and creates two objects. Note how the two object facts are reflected in the figure:

1. Because two separate object literals are evaluated, two *distinct* objects are created, even though each object contains the same properties with the same values.

2. Although the code seems to suggest the objects themselves are stored inside the variables, the variables contain only references.

The use of references means that one object can be simultaneously referred to by more than one variable. Either variable can be used to update the object's properties, and either can be used to see these updates. See Figure 4.2.

You can disassociate an object from a variable by assigning a different value to the variable. The special value `null` is particularly useful in this regard. It's generally used to represent the notion of a "pointer to nothing," as shown in Figure 4.3.

Every object you create takes up storage space. When an object ceases to be referenced from any variable, it becomes known as *garbage*. JavaScript garbage eventually gets picked up, freeing up the storage space it occupied for you to create new objects. Generating garbage is a good thing; it's a bad thing to hold on to objects you will never use again, as that space will never be freed up. A program that loses memory because unused objects are not being reclaimed is said to have a *memory leak*.

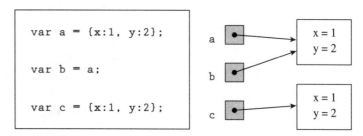

Figure 4.1 Three variables and two objects

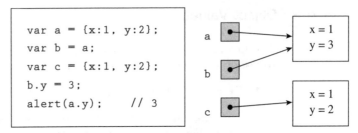

Figure 4.2 Updating a property of a shared object

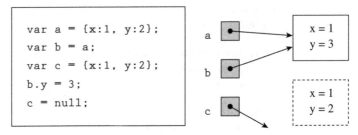

Figure 4.3 Assigning null to a variable

4.3 Prototypes

Consider a script that deals with thousands of points on the Earth's surface. A function that creates points would free us from writing object literals for every point, each of which would need to repeat the words "latitude" and "longitude." We might try this script:

```javascript
// This function creates a new point every time it is called.
var make_point = function(lat, lon) {
    return {
        latitude: lat,
        longitude: lon,
        is_valid: function() {
            return Math.abs(this.latitude) <= 90 &&
                Math.abs(this.longitude) <= 180;
        },
        antipode: function() {
            return make_point(-this.latitude, -this.longitude);
        },
        is_in_arctic_circle: function() { return this.latitude > 66.5608; }
    };
};

// Example calls
var mauna_kea = make_point(19.8210, -155.4683);
```

```
alert(mauna_kea.is_in_arctic_circle());    // Alerts false.
alert(mauna_kea.is_valid());               // Alerts true.
var north_pole = make_point(90, 0);
alert(north_pole.is_in_arctic_circle());   // Alerts true.
alert(north_pole.antipode().latitude);     // Alerts -90.
```

Of course, this code is terribly wasteful. Every point object we create requires space to store all five fields (even though the functions are meant to be shared), and each object gets its own copy of the three functions (see Figure 4.4).

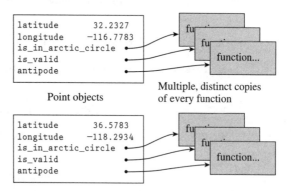

Figure 4.4   Wasteful copies of property values

Fortunately, the designers of JavaScript realized the need for similar objects to share properties. For this reason, they gave every object a special hidden property that is (either `null` or) a reference to another object called its *prototype*. Whenever you try to read a nonexistent property of an object, JavaScript will look for the property in the prototype object. If the property isn't there, the prototype of the prototype is searched, and so on. Figure 4.5 shows a single prototype holding the shared properties for our points.

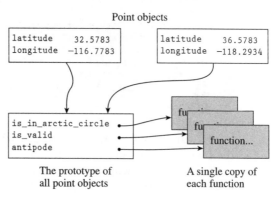

Figure 4.5   Objects sharing a prototype

JavaScript attaches the prototype to an object at the time the object is created. Let's see how this is done.

4.4 Constructors

As mentioned earlier, JavaScript functions are objects. Every function has (at least) two properties: `length`, the number of parameters in its declaration, and `prototype`, the object that will be attached to all objects created with this function, provided the function was called with the operator `new`. When a function is called this way (e.g., `new Point(...)`) JavaScript does some magic:

1. It creates a brand-new object.

2. It sets the prototype of this new object to the value of the function's `prototype` property.

3. It executes the function, with the value of `this` being the new object.

4. It returns the new object from the function unless you explicitly return something else.

Functions intended to be used with `new` are called *constructors*. The convention for creating new types of things (such as points) is to write a constructor that fills in properties unique to each object instance, while putting into the prototype properties that are shared. For points, we can define and use the following constructor:

```
var Point = function(lat, lon) {
    this.latitude = lat;
    this.longitude = lon;
};

Point.prototype.is_in_arctic_circle = function() {
    return this.latitude > 66.5608;
};
Point.prototype.antipode = function() {
    return make_point(-this.latitude, -this.longitude);
};
Point.prototype.is_valid = function() {
    return Math.abs(this.latitude) <= 90 &&
           Math.abs(this.longitude) <= 180;
};
```

Be careful not to confuse the `prototype` property of the function with the function's own prototype. Remember—the value of `Point.prototype` is the object that will be attached as the prototype for all objects *created with* the call `new Point(...)`.

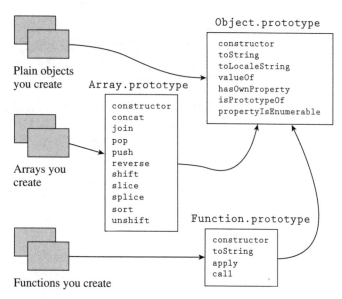

Figure 4.6 Object, function, and array prototypes

Let's see the new type in action:

```
var p = new Point(40.185486, 44.515069);
alert(p.is_in_arctic_circle());   // Alerts false.
```

Objects created with curly braces ({...}), internally call **new Object()**, so these objects have a prototype of **Object.prototype**. Creating an array object (with [...]) calls **new Array()**, so an array's prototype is **Array.prototype**. Similarly, all function objects receive **Function.prototype**. These "built-in" prototypes are used to store properties common to all objects, arrays, and functions, respectively. Also, because prototypes *are* objects themselves, they have prototype properties, too. All except **Object.prototype**, that is—it is designed to be the ultimate prototype. See Figure 4.6.

Because **Object.prototype** sits at the end of every prototype chain, its functions are available to every object.[1] The **hasOwnProperty** and **toString** properties are the most widely used. The former returns a Boolean value indicating whether there is a property with the given name in the object itself (not the prototype!); the latter returns a string representation of the object.

---

1. Unless some clever (or malicious) programmer has manipulated the prototype chain.

```
var p = new Point(40.185486, 44.515069);
alert(p.hasOwnProperty("latitude"));     // Alerts true.
alert(p.hasOwnProperty("antipode"));     // Alerts false.
alert(p.toString());                     // Alerts [object Object].
```

Whoops! The last alert sure was ugly. But we can fix this by giving `Point.prototype` its own `toString` property. This will allow points to display nicely, without affecting the way other objects are displayed (see Exercise 9 at the end of this chapter):

```
Point.prototype.toString = function() {
    return "(" + Math.abs(this.latitude) +
        (this.latitude > 0 ? "N" : "S") + "," +
        Math.abs(this.longitude) +
        (this.longitude > 0 ? "E" : "W") + ")";
};
var p = new Point(40.185486, 44.515069);
alert(p.toString());                // Alerts (40.185486N,44.515069E)
```

The `toString` property is actually quite special. Try this function call:

```
alert(p);
```

Here `p` is a point and `alert` expects a string. In JavaScript, when a string is expected but an object is supplied, the object's `toString` property is called.

The `hasOwnProperty` function is generally used in conjunction with the variant of the `for` statement (sometimes called the for-in statement) that iterates through all of an object's properties, often including those in the object's prototype.

```
var point = new Point(0, 0);
// alerts latitude, longitude, antipode, is_in_arctic_circle, etc.
for (var p in point) {
    alert(p);
}
```

Many scripts will want to exclude properties from the prototype, so the following idiom is the most common choice:

```
var point = new Point(0, 0);
// Alerts latitude and longitude only.
for (var p in point) {
    if (point.hasOwnProperty(p)) {
        alert(p);
    }
}
```

4.5 Native, Built-In, and Host Objects

JavaScript programs are designed to run inside some *host environment*, such as a cell phone, web browser, Adobe Acrobat, or Adobe Photoshop. Objects you create in a JavaScript program, as well as a handful of *built-in* objects, are called *native objects*. Objects provided by the host environment are called *host objects*. Web browsers, for instance, supply host objects such as windows, documents, buttons, cookies, frames, browsing histories, menus, text fields, and many more. You'll see some of these in the next chapter.

Among the few dozen built-in JavaScript objects are `Object`, `Function`, `Math`, `Number`, `Boolean`, `String`, `Date`, `Array`, `RegExp`, and `Error`.[2] One of the more useful of these objects is the constructor function `Date`. The expression `new Date()` creates a date object for the current time. If necessary, you may then modify properties of the date (e.g., the month or year) by calling functions such as `setMonth` and `setYear`.

```
var d = new Date();
d.setFullYear("2285");
d.setMonth(5);
d.setDate(20);
d.setHours(18);
d.setMinutes(29);
alert(d);
```

For this code, we got the following alert (your output may differ):

```
Sat Jun 20 2285 18:29:54 GMT-0700 (PDT)
```

Note the month value. JavaScript uses 0 through 11—beware!

4.6 Regular Expressions*

A *regular expression*, or *regex*, is a pattern representing a set of strings. JavaScript regexes are generally delimited with slashes (/ ... /). We usually speak of a regex as *matching* strings. For example:

- `/dog|rat|cat/` matches any string containing "dog" or "rat" or "cat," because the "|" character means *or*.
- `/colou?r/` matches any string containing "color" or "colour," because the question mark means *optional*.

---

2. The complete list of built-ins, and their properties and behavior, can be found in [ECM99].

- /go*gle/ matches any string containing "ggle," "gogle," "google," "gooogle," "goooogle," and so on, because the asterisk means *zero or more*. The plus sign is related; it means *one or more*: /go+gle/ will not match "ggle," for example.

- /b[aeiou]b/ matches any string containing "bab," "beb," "bib," "bob," or "bub," because the square brackets mean *one of*.

- /^Once/ matches any string *beginning with* "Once" (indicated by the caret).

- /ss$/ matches any string *ending with* "ss" (indicated by the dollar sign).

- /^dog$/ matches any string that begins and ends with "dog"—in other words, it matches *only* the string "dog".

- /^[A-PR-Y0-9]{10}$/ matches only a string of 10 characters, each of which is an uppercase letter A through P or R through Y, or a decimal digit.

- /^z{3,5}$/ matches "zzz," "zzzz," and "zzzzz."

- /\s\d+\s/ matches a string containing a whitespace character followed by one or more decimal digits 0 . . . 9 followed by a whitespace character.

The `test` function on regexes will tell you whether a regex matches a string, whereas the `search` function on strings will return the position in the string of the first match. You can also use regexes when splitting strings or replacing pieces of strings.

```
/ab\s+cd?/.test("tab  characters")  ⇒ true
/^[0-9]+/.test("U2 - War")          ⇒ false
"JavaScript".search(/[N-Z]/)        ⇒ 4
"Brendan".search(/x+/)              ⇒ -1
"ladedada".split(/ad/)              ⇒ ["l","ed","a"]
"Hello".replace(/[ei]/, "u")        ⇒ "Hullo"
```

The Regex constructor is required when the pattern depends on data not known until the script is running:

```
var name = prompt("What's your name?");
var pattern = new Regex("^" + name + "$");
```

Can you see why writing /^name$/ would be wrong?

A full treatment of regular expressions requires far more space than is available in this short guide. You can, for instance, *capture* the piece of the string matched by the regex using the `match` and `exec` functions. Special pattern characters such as ?= and ?! allow matching if and only if the matched string is, or is not, followed by some given pattern. Taking the time to master regular expressions will pay many dividends. Well-chosen regexes can turn 100 lines of code into fewer than 10.

4.7 The Global Object

Every JavaScript environment has a single, unique object known as the *global object*. For those interested in the technical aspects of the language:

1. Top-level variables are really properties of the global object.

2. The global object appears at the end of every scope chain, meaning it is searched last when looking up variables.

In fact, the scope chains in Figures 3.3 through 3.5 can now be understood to be objects in their own right, with the global object being found at the end of the chain. Variables and parameters of a function are properties of the function's activation object.

The global object actually contains a fair number of properties when JavaScript starts up. Among these are `NaN`, `Infinity`, `isNaN`, `isFinite`, `undefined`, `escape`, `unescape`, `parseInt`, `parseFloat`, `Object`, `Array`, `Function`, `Date`, `Boolean`, and all the rest of what we have been calling the built-in constructors.

The built-in objects, then, are simply properties of the built-in global object. You don't usually think about this fact because you never mention the global object when referring to its properties. However—and here is where things get really interesting—JavaScript environments are allowed to augment the global object with anything they like. In most Web environments, the global object contains dozens of properties. For example, `document` is a reference to the innards of the containing web page; `screen` is a reference to a screen object describing the screen size and available colors; `alert` is a function that pops up a message box; and so on. There's even a property of the global object called `window` whose value is—get this—a reference to the global object itself! This means you *can* write

```
window.window.window.window.window.window.alert("Hi");
```

...but doesn't mean you should.

There is a great deal more on the `window` object and host objects in Chapter 5, where we write scripts that live and run within a web browser.

Chapter Summary

- Objects consist of properties, which contain values. Property values can be, and often are, other objects.

- Object values are actually references, so the exact same object can be referred to by multiple variables at the same time.

- Every object contains a hidden reference to another object, called its prototype. When a request for a property is made on an object and the object doesn't have that property, the request is sent to the prototype.

- A constructor creates a new object and assigns its prototype.

- A JavaScript environment consists of native objects and host objects. The built-in objects are a subset of the native objects.

Exercises

1. Let p = { x: 1, y: [4, {z: 2}] }. What is p.y[1]?

2. What is the value of { x: 1, y: 2 }.y? Would you ever write something like that?

3. What is the difference between p["dog"] and p[dog]?

4. Write a function that takes in a song object, like the example in Section 4.1, and returns its duration in *minutes*. The duration stored in the object is in seconds.

5. Write a function that takes in an array of song objects and returns the cumulative duration of all of the songs, in seconds.

6. How many objects are created by the following for statement?

```
for (var i = 0; i < 100; i++) {
    alert({ x: 1, y: 2 });
}
```

7. Given the point constructor in Section 4.3, write code that creates a point object, then assigns an integer value to its toString property. What happens when you call alert with this object? (You will need to try this code out; the answer is not in the text.)

8. Write a constructor function suitable for constructing song objects like the song in the example in Section 4.1.

9. Explain why adding toString to Point.prototype does not affect the way objects other than points are converted to strings.

10. Suppose your friend expresses annoyance with having to type the word `Math` in front of every mathematical function, and decides to declare a number of top-level variables like this: `var sin = Math.sin;` `var cos = Math.cos; var log = Math.log;` and so on. What do you tell your friend?

11. Make a list of the properties of the global object in the JavaScript environment of your favorite browser and operating system.

12. Explain why `window.window.window.window.window.alert("Hi")` works, in your own words.

Interaction

Thus far, your scripts have communicated with their users exclusively via `prompt` when requesting input and via `alert` when displaying output. As with any language, user interaction with JavaScript can be accomplished in other ways; of these, the most popular by far is the Web. Now that you are better acquainted with the language, we can discuss web page interaction more effectively.

Because JavaScript and the Web are very tightly coupled in most people's minds, you might have expected a chapter such as this to appear sooner in the book. We have purposely delayed discussing web technologies to this point because we believe that maximizing JavaScript's potential with the Web involves understanding JavaScript *as a programming language* first. Thus this chapter has a second purpose: It is also intended to bring the material from previous chapters together, like individual puzzle pieces that can now form a meaningful picture.

5.1 Phone Numbers Revisited

Taken in isolation, the phone number scripts introduced in Chapter 1 are not ready for prime time: The only way to invoke them is to copy/paste or type the code into some scratch page, and then have that page run the script. It certainly isn't fair to ask this of your potential user base; they expect the scripts to be part of a web page with a convenient user interface, a simple version of which is shown in Figure 5.1. The screenshot on the left displays the page when it is loaded for the first time. The view on the right displays the page after some input into the text field and some "dialing" on the virtual keypad.

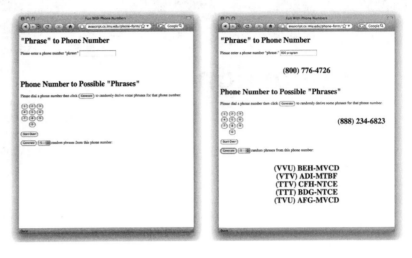

(a) On initial load   (b) After some user interaction

Figure 5.1 A simple web-based interface for phone number conversions

Visit `http://javascript.cs.lmu.edu/phone-form` to interact with the page for yourself. The application consists of two files: `phone-form.html` and `phoneConversion.js`. When you view the page's source, you are seeing `phone-form.html`. To see the `phoneConversion.js` file, access `http://javascript.cs.lmu.edu/js/phoneConversion.js`.

Take a moment to read the code in `phoneConversion.js`. Note its overall structure; it is essentially a list of function definitions. As part of good programming practice, there are comments aplenty. The function code itself includes constructs from previous chapters: variables, different kinds of statements and operators, objects, arrays, and even advanced features such as regular expressions.

The rest of this chapter describes the technology behind these kinds of dynamic web pages, making full use of the language elements discussed so far. We conclude by introducing Ajax, a combination of JavaScript and dynamic web pages with behind-the-scenes data exchange to produce highly interactive, yet efficient web applications.

5.2 Dynamic HTML

Web pages are written in *Hypertext Markup Language* (*HTML*). They are delivered over the Internet by web servers to web browsers, then *rendered* by these browsers into the visual representations with which we are so familiar. Without JavaScript, these pages are *static*—that is, once loaded, their content will not change. The only way to change the display is to click on a link, which effectively restarts the connect-and-render cycle for a new web page. With JavaScript, the web page gains the ability to trigger *changes to itself*, thus becoming *dynamic* based on the user's interaction with the content on that page.

(While prior knowledge of HTML is not absolutely necessary at this point, it may be helpful nonetheless. You might want to have one or more HTML tutorials or references handy, on paper or on screen. A quick web search should yield an abundance of such resources.)

The key to JavaScript's facilitation of *dynamic HTML* is its ability to access and manipulate a web page's content in a manner that is identical to accessing and manipulating any other object or function. A web browser, its window(s), and its HTML documents are *exposed* to JavaScript in the form of well-defined, built-in objects. Scripts can access the information in these objects just as they would any other JavaScript object described in the previous chapters. Changes to these objects result in immediate, sometimes visible, effects. For a quick demonstration of just such an effect, type and run the following code into the scratch page:

```
document.getElementById("introduction").style.background = "red";
```

Despite not having seen an explanation of this code yet, can you still see a correlation between what happened and what you typed and ran? From a language perspective, you can tell this much: A function called **getElementById**, defined for some object called **document**, returns some other object, which has a property called **style**, which in turn has a property called **background**. The value **"red"** is then assigned to this **background** property. The rub, of course, is what *is* this function? What are these properties? What do they have to do with the web page?

The objects, functions, and properties that were used in the previous one-liner, and many more, are collectively known as the *document object model (DOM)*. The DOM serves as the central technology that enables dynamic HTML.[1]

5.2.1 The Document Is "Just" a Built-In Object

From a language point of view, the DOM is a set of built-in objects and functions, no different from the likes of **Math**, **Date**, **prompt**, and **alert**. What makes the DOM interesting is its direct connection to visible elements such as the web browser, its windows, and the content within these windows. Thus, while a document is, as stated in this section's title, "just"

---

1. A full discussion of HTML is beyond the scope of this book; our assumption is that you at least recognize how HTML consists of a set of nested tags with accompanying attributes.

another built-in object, it is probably the most complex object in the bunch. In addition, because the DOM serves as the liaison between web page users and JavaScript's functionality, it includes the concept of *events*, which represent things that "happen" outside the explicit activity in your JavaScript code. Events include actions taken by a user on the current web page or even background activity performed by the web browser, such as something that you might have scheduled for advance or periodic execution or even incoming data over the network.

The rudimentary scratch page at `http://javascript.cs.lmu.edu/ scratch` is itself a web page and, therefore, is visible as a JavaScript object. Type this into the scratch page and run it:

```
alert(document);
```

What do you see? You see an `alert` dialog box, of course, but what does it contain? It certainly isn't `null` or `undefined`. Thus, at the very least, `document` is a bona fide, predefined object. The `alert` message tells you precisely that.

Because `document` is a built-in object, it must have properties. To see some of them, enter and run this script:

```
var i = 0;
for (var property in document) {
    alert(property);
    i = i + 1;
    if (i > 4) {
        break;
    }
}
```

You should see a sequence of five `alert` dialogs, each with a name such as `bgColor`, `width`, or `getElementById`. We can't give you a definitive list here, because different browsers may list `document`'s properties in different orders (they may even include properties that other browsers won't have). But note how, code-wise, this is *exactly* how you would iterate through the properties of any old JavaScript object.

The `i` counter in the preceding script limits the number of properties shown to five; without it, you would have to press *Enter* or *Return* quite a number of times. There is, however, a more palatable way to view all of `document`'s properties. Try this script:

```
var footer = document.getElementById("footer");
footer.innerHTML = "<b>document properties:</b><br/>";
for (var property in document) {
    footer.innerHTML += property + "<br/>";
}
```

Figure 5.2 The JavaScript scratch page, with a script that has appended document's properties to its content

What happens now? You should see something that's not unlike Figure 5.2. Your script has *changed the actual content of the scratch page*. This is the essence of dynamic HTML—changes to document are immediately manifested as changes to the browser window. This capability represents a potential replacement for the venerable alert function.

The DOM "object zoo" does not stop with document or its immediate properties. What lies beneath is an entire *tree* of objects, with document at the top. And if you are familiar with HTML, it gets even better: The structure of this tree *parallels the structure of the web page's HTML source.* Figure 5.3 illustrates this structure for our now-familiar JavaScript scratch page. Individual elements of the tree (e.g., document, p, form) are called *nodes*; when a DOM node contains additional nodes (e.g., head contains meta and title), the containing node is a *parent* node, while the contained nodes are the parent's *children*. A child node may have only one parent; document, the only node that has no parents is called the *root* of the tree.

How about a replacement for prompt? If adding content to a web page corresponds to displaying output, then it makes sense that *reading* the user-editable sections of a page, such as text areas, check boxes, radio buttons, lists, and more, would correspond to receiving input. In fact, this is the case. Try this script:

```
var scriptArea = document.getElementById("scriptArea");
var footer = document.getElementById("footer");
footer.innerHTML = "<pre>" + scriptArea.value + "</pre>";
```

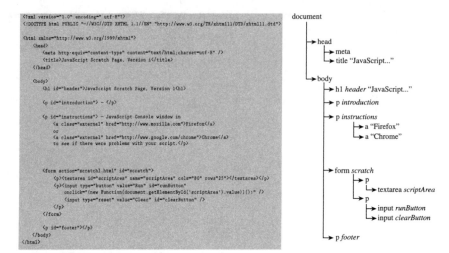

Figure 5.3 HTML and `document` representations of the JavaScript scratch page, with paragraph text elided for brevity; note the parallels between HTML tags and `document`'s properties (and the properties of *its* properties, etc.)

When you run this script, you should find that the web page has been appended with something that looks almost exactly like the content of the scratch page's text area. That's because it *is* the content of the scratch page's text area—you have just asked JavaScript to access that text and then copy it to the bottom of the page (also known as the page's "footer")!

The script has replaced `prompt` with another mechanism for receiving information from the user; specifically, it reads the content of the scratch page's text area. The rudimentary scratch page has one other such mechanism: the *Run* button. The ability to click a button counts as user input.

One last thing before we move on: When we say that the DOM exposes everything on a web page to JavaScript manipulation, we do mean *everything*. This following script demonstrates this flexibility—even buttons, whose content is typically sacrosanct in most other environments (or else not changeable on the fly), are fair game in the DOM:

```
var runButton = document.getElementById("runButton");
runButton.value = "Please Execute This Script as Soon as Possible";
```

But why stop there? You can never have too many buttons:

```
var form = document.getElementById("scratch");
var newButton = document.createElement("input");
newButton.type = "button";
newButton.value = "I'm New!  But I Do Nothing...";
form.appendChild(newButton);
```

(Needless to say, you really should type and run these things to get the most out of what you're reading—there are no screenshots here to let you off the hook.)

5.2.2   Elements and IDs for Fun and Profit

HTML defines a large number of objects beyond those illustrated in our rudimentary scratch page. To introduce you to more DOM elements without requiring you to write entire web pages from scratch, we move to a new scratch page that includes more objects to manipulate. This page can be seen in Figure 5.4 and is accessible online at `http://javascript.cs.lmu.edu/playground`.

Figure 5.4 A JavaScript scratch page with more DOM elements that you can manipulate

Before we dive further into this new page, let's demystify some of the properties that we have used so far. The top-level `document` object (Figure 5.3) has the following functions:

`getElementById(`*name*`)`: This function locates and returns, as a JavaScript object, the page element whose `id` attribute in HTML has been set to *name*.

`createElement(`*type*`)`: This function creates a new HTML element, as if the tag specified in *type* were written into the original HTML file. The new element does not get added to the page yet (the function `appendChild` does that), so you can think of that element as existing in a "holding area" as you customize its properties further.

All dynamic HTML activity typically starts with a call to `document` `.getElementById`, so as to "get to" the DOM node that you want to manipulate. This manipulation then involves reading or writing properties such as the following:

`innerHTML`: This property, which is available for nodes that correspond to HTML blocks such as `<p> ... </p>` or `<div> ... </div>`, represents the exact HTML code that appears within that block's opening and closing tags. Assigning a new value to this property results in an immediate change to the corresponding section of the web page.

`value`: This property, which is available for most nodes that solicit user input, represents the current content of that element, such as the text within a text field, the state of a radio button, or the current selection in a list. As with `innerHTML`, assigning something to this property immediately modifies the corresponding element in the web page.

DOM nodes within `document` also have functions of their own; of these, we have used only `appendChild(`*newElement*`)`. This function adds *newElement* to the invoked DOM node's list of children. It's equivalent to inserting a new HTML tag into a page's HTML source, within the tag that corresponds to the invoked DOM node.

So far, we have described three functions and two properties. While these are likely to be the functions and properties that you will use most often, a *lot* more is available in the DOM. For a more comprehensive list, web searches such as "JavaScript DOM properties" or "JavaScript DOM reference" should yield sites that contain this information. Popular sites include those hosted at `http://www.w3schools.com/js/js_obj_htmldom.asp`, `http://www.mozilla.org/docs/dom`, and finally the authoritative standard defined by the World Wide Web Consortium (W3C) at `http://www.w3.org/DOM`. Most of these sites have a search function or outline that is based on the actual object, function, and property names within the DOM, such as the handful just listed.

We're ready to start working with our new playground page. The key to reaching the element (tag) that you want is to use `getElementById`. But, as they say, with this power comes a responsibility: The HTML source must make sure that the elements you'll want *have* IDs assigned to them in the first place. This is a key aspect of the HTML–JavaScript symbiosis: For JavaScript to get to (and manipulate) the web page easily, the web page must be marked up with identifiers for the tags that the scripts will care about.

It's easy to spot the IDs in a web page. While viewing our new page in a browser, select that browser's *View Source*, *Page Source*, or a similarly named command. This opens a new window showing the HTML code for the web page. Every tag with an `id` attribute (e.g., `<p id="description">`) is an element that you can reach using `getElementById`.

Take a moment to get to know the ID'ed tags in the page, and then type in this script:

```
// Grab the elements that we need.
var input1 = document.getElementById("input1");
var input2 = document.getElementById("input2");
var status = document.getElementById("status");

// Read the required values.
var number1 = parseFloat(input1.value);
var number2 = parseFloat(input2.value);

// Write the result.
status.innerHTML = number1 + " + " + number2 + " = " + (number1 + number2);
```

You've just written a simple adder![2] The script grabs the `input1` and `input2` text fields from the page, converts the text within those fields (their `value` property) into numbers via the built-in `parseFloat` function, and adds the resulting numbers together. While addition itself may be trivial, this script is meant to show you how judicious assignment of IDs to HTML elements makes it extremely easy, with the help of `getElementById`, to access and modify the content of a web page—including content that solicits user input, such as the input fields.

---

2. Of course, the correctness of this adder is subject to the correctness of JavaScript arithmetic in general, as discussed in Chapter 2.

Of course, the labeling and information on the page doesn't really say "adder," so let's tweak the web page accordingly with this script:

```
document.getElementById("header").innerHTML =
    "A Simple Dynamic HTML Adder";

document.getElementById("introduction").innerHTML =
    "This page adds two numbers.";

document.getElementById("instructions").innerHTML =
    "Type a number into each of the fields below, " +
    "paste the addition script into the text area, " +
    "then click the <i>Add</i> button.";

document.getElementById("input1Label").innerHTML = "Addend 1";
document.getElementById("input2Label").innerHTML = "Addend 2";
document.getElementById("status").innerHTML = "";
document.getElementById("runButton").value = "Add 'Em";

// Make everything else invisible.
var idsToHide = [ "check", "checkLabel", "row2", "row3" ];
for (var index = 0; index < idsToHide.length; index += 1) {
    document.getElementById(idsToHide[index]).style.display = "none";
}

// A final reminder that we need the separate adder script
// pasted in.
alert("Don't forget to paste/type in the adder script!");
```

Once this script is run, replace it with the pure addition script. Note how the changes "stick" for as long as you don't refresh the page. The JavaScript objects that you've manipulated stay with the page until a new one is read into the browser's window. Web pages bookend JavaScript's "life span:" Objects, variables, functions, and everything else are all discarded when a web page is closed, refreshed, or replaced, to be taken over by whatever DOM/scripts/variables appear in the next page.

The following collection of one-liners shows how you aren't restricted to just text values or the innerHTML property; feel free to run just the ones that interest you the most. Sometimes a one-liner may affect more than one element. For example, selecting a radio button automatically de-selects another radio button. In addition, one of the lines has no immediate visible effect, but affects the behavior of some lines after it—can you identify this line?

```
document.getElementById("input1").disabled = true;
document.getElementById("check").disabled = true;
document.getElementById("check").checked = true;
document.getElementById("radio2").checked = true;
// The radio buttons are mutually exclusive.
document.getElementById("radio4").checked = true;
document.getElementById("password").value = "swordfish";
document.getElementById("password").readOnly = true;
```

```
document.getElementById("category").selectedIndex = 2;
document.getElementById("category").style["vertical-align"] = "bottom";
document.getElementById("wonder").multiple = true;
document.getElementById("wonder").style.float = "right";
document.getElementById("wonder").options[1].selected = true;
document.getElementById("wonder").options[3].selected = true;
document.getElementById("status").style.border = "medium outset #0f0";
document.getElementById("status").style["text-align"] = "right";
```

You may have noticed that properties that are purely visual—those affecting only the *appearance* of an HTML element (e.g., color, fonts, borders, margins, visibility), and not its data or behavior (e.g., checked/unchecked, enabled/disabled)—are reached through an intermediary `style` property. These properties pertain to a distinct standard called *Cascading Style Sheets (CSS)*. Unfortunately, CSS by itself is a whole additional ball of wax, and so is beyond the scope of this book. For now, you can get by in terms of learning it by just making sure to include "CSS" as a search term when looking for information about a web content property that pertains only to appearance. The authoritative CSS home page is `http://www.w3.org/Style/CSS`.

Before moving on, take a moment to appreciate that there truly is a seemingly endless number of objects and properties within the DOM. One way to gain proficiency with these things is to find what is available (via books and online references) and experiment by manipulating these properties on some page with known content and IDs, such as our playground page. It's safe to change, add, and delete things as much as you like, because everything you do dynamically goes quietly away once you close the window or visit another website.

5.2.3 Events

Now that you've seen how scripts can read, write, and otherwise have total control over the content of a web page, a chicken-and-egg question may have emerged in your mind: Who runs the scripts? With the scratch pages so far, you write up the code and then click *Run*. In practice, of course, that's not how it's done. Scripts just "happen." This section discusses precisely how these scripts happen, using HTML/JavaScript's event mechanism.

An *event* is a term for something that may happen during the life of a program, outside of the code that is currently being executed. If a program cares about a particular event—for example, it may need to respond to mouse clicks—then an *event handler* is set up for that event. The handler is nothing fancy; it is simply a function. What distinguishes event handlers from other functions is that, once set up, they are called "automatically"[3] when an event takes place.

---

3. Yes, you guessed it—there's more to this topic than can be said within the scope of this book.

Most of the time, events refer to actions performed by a user. For example, mouse activity triggers "mouse events," keyboard actions trigger "key events," and so on. If you think about it, such user activity is, indeed, a good fit for events: Users can move or click the mouse at any time, press keys at any time, or do anything else at any time. Thus the only way for your program to respond to such activities is through an event handler. There *are* non-user-triggered events, though; you'll read about a particularly useful one in Section 5.3. But for now, let's stick with things that a user might do.

The page `http://javascript.cs.lmu.edu/playground` does not, by default, handle any events in a custom way. Let's add a trivial event handler just to get things started:

```
document.getElementById("header").onclick =
                              function() { alert(this.innerHTML); };
```

When you run this script, nothing will seem to happen. Something *has* happened, however: The page has been told to handle *click* events on the page element whose ID is `header`. This element happens to be the large heading of the page—click on it now and see what happens.

Simple, but perhaps not too useful. Here's something that you are more likely to see "in the wild." Again, type it into `http://javascript. cs.lmu.edu/playground` and then run the script:

```
/*
 * Enables or disables the category drop-down menu.
 */
var setCategoryEnabled = function(enabled) {
    // Recall that "!" in JavaScript means "not."
    document.getElementById("category").disabled = !enabled;
};

/*
 * Enables or disables the category drop-down menu based
 * on whether the "Check me" box is checked.
 */
var handleCheckClick = function() {
    setCategoryEnabled(this.checked);
};

// Sync up the drop-down menu and the check box.
setCategoryEnabled(document.getElementById("check").checked);

// Set the event handler.
document.getElementById("check").onclick = handleCheckClick;
```

After running this script, clicking on the check box, which corresponds to toggling its `checked` property, will enable or disable the *Category* drop-down menu accordingly, via its `disabled` property. `handleCheckClick` is the event handler for the [mouse] *click* event of the check box. This particular event handler illustrates another distinct property of these functions: When invoked by an event, some properties have preassigned values. `this` is set to refer to the DOM element that triggered that event, so we can use `this.checked` without calling `getElementById` first. Also, though not used in this example, `event` is set to an object representing the event itself. These *event objects* hold supplementary information about the event that just took place. The information that is available depends on the event type. With a mouse event, for example, you might want to know the mouse coordinates of the event. For a key event, you might want to know if the *Shift* key was being held down at the time. You can look up dynamic HTML/DOM/JavaScript reference sites for comprehensive lists of the events that are available and the information that they provide in their corresponding event objects.

Here's another script that shows off a few more standard events, including access to the aforementioned `event` object from within an event handler invocation:

```
/* Eliminates all nondigits from the given string. */
var restrictToDigits = function(string) {
    return string.replace(/[^\d]/g, "");
};

/* Checks if the given value is all digits. */
var isAllDigits = function(string) {
    return string.match(/^\d*$/);
};

/* Rejects nondigit keypresses. */
var handleInputKeyPress = function() {
    // Yes, this is slight overkill because we are sure to have
    // a one-character string, but it still works.
    if (!isAllDigits(String.fromCharCode(event.charCode))) {
        event.preventDefault();
    }
};

/* Rejects nondigits in this.value, and reselects the text field. */
var handleInputBlur = function() {
    if (!isAllDigits(this.value)) {
        alert("Sorry, only 0-9 are allowed here.");
        this.value = restrictToDigits(this.value);
        this.select();
    }
};
```

```
document.getElementById("input1").onkeypress = handleInputKeyPress;
document.getElementById("input2").onblur = handleInputBlur;
```

After running this script, try typing values into the page's *Input 1* and *Input 2* fields. If all went well, *Input 1* should now accept only digits 0 to 9, with all other characters being rejected. The way that this task is accomplished reveals a new aspect of the event mechanism: *event propagation*. "Normal" button clicks, text field edits, and other activity are actually done by event handlers, too—they are *default* handlers that are automatically "installed" in the DOM nodes. Further, elements can reside within elements—a parent element may have an event handler for some event, but its child does not. This is where *propagation* comes into play: When triggered, an event is passed to a custom handler first, if available. After the custom handler comes the default handler for that "closest" element; when there is no default handler (such as for elements that are typically "inert," including paragraphs or headings), the event then goes to the element's parent, and so on, until either *something* deals with it or the root of the DOM tree is reached.

There are additional details and caveats to event propagation (particularly with regard to differences among browsers), but as with other areas, this book is not the place for them. The bottom line is that more than one handler, whether assigned by a script or installed by default, has the opportunity to respond to an event.

For text input fields, the default handler for keypresses inserts the character represented by the pressed key into the field. In the case of our digit restricter, we don't always want this to happen; we want only *digits* to be entered into the text field. That's where the `preventDefault` function comes in. Calling this function tells JavaScript to "stop right here"—in other words, don't *propagate* the event to the default event handler. Thus, when our custom handler catches nondigits, `preventDefault()` treats them like they never happened (from the point of view of the default keypress event handler for *Input 1*).

Input 2 will also accept only digits 0 to 9, but checks for conformity with this criterion only after you tab out of that field or click on another control. If the value in *Input 2* contains anything other than 0–9, you'll get an `alert` message to that effect when the field loses *focus* (i.e., it stops being the target of keypresses). A change in focus (i.e., becoming or ceasing to be the recipient of keypresses) is as much an event as a mouse click or a key hit. When an element receives focus (e.g., it's "tabbed into" or clicked on), the `onfocus` event takes place. When an element *loses* focus (e.g., it's "tabbed out of" or another element is clicked), dynamic HTML engages in a little word play by invoking `onblur` (i.e., the opposite of "focus" is "blur"—get it?).

Of course, you (almost) never see event handling assigned by user-entered code that gets run. Instead, the dynamic web pages that we use "just know" how to handle events. In substance, such pages aren't doing anything differently from what you just did. Instead, the little event scripts are already included as part of the web page's files, including an option to encode them as attributes of HTML tags.

To see event handling that is set up directly within the page's HTML source, visit `http://javascript.cs.lmu.edu/boxes`. This page displays a number of HTML boxes that you can drag around. They also "light up" as your mouse rolls over them. If you view the HTML source of `boxes.html`, you'll see tags like these:

```
<div id="box1"
    class="box"
    style="left: 100px; top: 100px; width: 200px; height: 150px;"
    onmouseover="highlight(this);"
    onmouseout="unhighlight(this);"
    onmousedown="startMove(this, event);"
    onmousemove="move(this, event);"
    onmouseup="endMove();">Hello world!</div>
```

These tags show how event handler scripts can be written into the HTML source. Every known user interface event has a corresponding HTML attribute, such as `onclick`, `onmousedown`, `onmouseover`, `onkeydown`, and many more, whose content or value is expected to be JavaScript code. When a user does something to an HTML element (e.g., holds down a mouse button over it), the web browser checks whether that action has been associated with a script via the corresponding on-whatever attribute. If such a script exists, it is invoked, after which the event is propagated for default handling (e.g., filling a text field, highlighting a selection) unless otherwise requested (recall `preventDefault` from a little earlier).

With events, dynamic HTML rounds out into a complete, self-contained package. When you access a dynamic HTML site, the web browser loads the HTML source. This source is displayed to the user as a web page, and is simultaneously exposed to JavaScript as the `document` object. As the user reads the web page, he or she may move the mouse, click somewhere, press a key, or do something else. If any of these events have been associated with a script, then the browser runs that script. More than likely, the script will access the DOM and manipulate it somehow, by changing some value or adding/removing elements. Once the script finishes, the user is back to looking at the web page, which is now different from the one that was originally read by the browser. And the cycle goes on, until the user requests a new web page. Then the cycle begins anew. These *event loops* go on ad infinitum, until the user quits the web browser.

5.2.4 Packaging a Dynamic HTML Website

While there is certainly much more beyond the material presented in this book, the core ideas of (1) the DOM for reading and/or writing the content of a web page directly, plus (2) events for responding to user activities within a web page, form the foundation of dynamic HTML. Before we go beyond this foundation, let's take a quick breather to examine the mechanics of how this HTML–JavaScript combination is delivered to a web browser.

In the previous section, event handlers were specified as JavaScript fragments set as attributes right within HTML tags. This is one way to get JavaScript "into" a web page. Two other mechanisms are also commonly used for this purpose:

■ Direct inclusion of JavaScript in the HTML content
■ Linking to a JavaScript file that is downloaded separately

Both mechanisms actually use the same HTML tag: `script`. Depending on how you use the tag, the browser either invokes JavaScript found right in the web page or loads a separate file and then runs it.

Here is the "direct inclusion" version of `script`:

```
<script type="text/javascript">
var displayMessage = function(message) {
    document.getElementById("message").innerHTML = message;
};
</script>
```

When the web browser gets to this part of the web page, it executes the included code. In this particular example, the result should be the definition of a `displayMessage` function. Subsequent `script` tags, as well as event handlers, will now be able to invoke this function as needed.

To reference a separate file, an `src` attribute is added to the `script` tag:

```
<script type="text/javascript" src="messageUtilities.js"></script>
```

Upon encountering this tag, the web browser will download JavaScript code in `messageUtilities.js` from the same location as the original HTML and then execute the content of that file. For example, if `messageUtilities.js` defines an `emailMessage` function, then that function will be defined as a result of loading the `messageUtilities.js` file. If `messageUtilities.js` defines a top-level `timestamp` variable, then that variable will be accessible to any other JavaScript code within that web page.

When a separate script file is given, `script`'s body is ignored. Don't bother doing this:

```
<script type="text/javascript" src="messageUtilities.js">
    var displayHelp = function() {
          alert("Please visit our support website."); };
</script>
```

In this case, the code in `messageUtilities.js` is downloaded and executed, but the code defining the `displayHelp` function is ignored, so `displayHelp` is never defined. Just break this up into separate script tags—you can include as many `script` tags as you like, of either type, within an HTML file. The browser treats all of those tags as if they were one big script whose code is executed in the order in which the tags appear.

These JavaScript inclusion mechanisms contribute to an overall JavaScript environment within which all subsequent scripts then run. Thus the typical JavaScript content of a dynamic HTML site, whether included directly in the HTML or loaded from separate files, consists mainly of function and variable definitions. As a page is loaded and rendered by the browser, these functions and variables cumulatively become available for access. When page loading finishes, user activity within that page triggers events that call those defined functions or access those variables as needed.

The built-up JavaScript environment remains valid until the next web page is loaded, either by the user clicking on a link or a reload of the same web page. Thus the `displayMessage` function defined in the earlier examples will exist for as long as the web browser stays on the page that defined it. If the browser loads a new page, that function goes away. If the browser reloads the page, then `displayMessage` remains available, but what really happened behind the scenes was that the "old" `displayMessage` function was discarded, and the page's `script` tag(s) defined it once more.

5.2.5 Other Related Built-In Objects

In addition to `document`, which is a JavaScript object representation of a web page's content and structure, other web browser-related JavaScript objects are available. We just list them here and leave full details to materials outside of this book:

`window` The window in which a web page is being displayed.

`navigator` The web browser application itself.

`screen` The user's display screen.

Using these objects is pretty much identical to using `document`—they're always available, you can read or write them by accessing their properties, and you can make them do things by accessing the functions that they define. The difference is that they are, after all, different objects, so the specific properties and functions that they have will be different from those in `document`. As always, look up more information on these objects to see all of the juicy details.

5.2.6 Timed or Ongoing Activity

For this last section on dynamic HTML, we present two functions that are not strictly related to the web environment, but are nonetheless very useful in giving web pages an active, "live" feel. These functions, `setTimeout` and `setInterval`, facilitate *deferred* or *ongoing* activity. In other words, they allow code to be run not at that exact point in a script, but rather at some point in the future or even at predefined intervals.

Enter this script into `http://javascript.cs.lmu.edu/playground`—but don't click *Run* right away:

```
var timeoutStr = document.getElementById("input1").value;
var timeout = parseFloat(timeoutStr) * 1000;
document.getElementById("status").innerHTML = "Wait for it...";
setTimeout(function()  document.getElementById('status').innerHTML =
    "Liftoff!"; , timeout);
```

Before running the program, enter a number, in seconds, into the *Input 1* text field. The green status area should change to *Wait for it ...* and should stay that way for the number of seconds that you entered. Then the message will change to *Liftoff!*

You have just used the `setTimeout` function to *defer* the calling of a JavaScript function for a specific number of milliseconds (thus explaining the preponderance of 1000s in this section's examples). `setTimeout` returns immediately, allowing your code to do other things while the deferred function "waits" in the background until the designated amount of time has elapsed. During that time, your code may have done a whole bunch of other things, including additional computation and handling events. To see this behavior in action, add an `alert` call right after the line with `setTimeout` and then run the script again. Note how the alert box appears immediately after you click *Run*, with *Liftoff!* appearing later (remember to type some number of seconds into *Input 1* so that things don't happen too quickly).

Now try this program:

```
setInterval(function()  document.getElementById('status').innerHTML =
    new Date(); , 1000);
```

This time, you're using `setInterval`. Like `setTimeout`, `setInterval` defers the calling of a function for some number of milliseconds. Unlike `setTimeout`, `setInterval` *repeats* the function call, between pauses (intervals) of the given amount of time. In the preceding example, the green status area of the playground page gets a by-the-second update of the current date and time. The function is called repeatedly, for, well ... almost forever. Without writing additional code, you'd need to reload a page, close the browser window, or visit a new site to end the repeated calls.

With additional code, you can exert better control over `setTimeout` and `setInterval`. When invoked, these functions actually return something—a value that serves as an *identifier* for the particular "deferred call" represented by the timeout or interval function. This identifier can subsequently be used in `clearTimeout` and `clearInterval`, respectively, to stop or cancel the pending function call(s). To use these functions, structure your code as shown here:

```
// When starting a timeout or interval, save the returned ID.
var timeoutID = setTimeout(someFunction, someDuration);
var intervalID = setInterval(anotherFunction, anotherDuration);

/* ...any other code runs here... */

// Whenever a timeout or interval must be canceled, invoke:
clearTimeout(timeoutID);
clearInterval(intervalID);
```

Visit `http://javascript.cs.lmu.edu/deferred` for a concrete demonstration of this family of functions. You can also use that web page to review the way HTML and JavaScript files are packaged, as discussed in Section 5.2.5.

At this point, you should have the information needed to fully understand the phone conversion page that was introduced in Section 5.1. Now would be a good time to revisit `http://javascript.cs.lmu.edu/phone-form` to see how the JavaScript interaction concepts described thus far come together to produce a relatively useful, and (we hope) fairly understandable, browser-based application.

When you're ready, we can go ahead and cap off this book with an introduction to Ajax, which combines JavaScript and dynamic HTML with the rest of the Web to realize the full interactive potential of each of these technologies.

5.3 Introduction to Ajax

Congratulations—you're almost done. Having come this far with this book, you should now know, among other things:

- The overall look (syntax) and meaning (semantics) of the JavaScript scripting/programming language (Chapters 1 to 4)
- The way a web browser "exposes" a web page's HTML content as a tree of JavaScript objects starting with `document` (Section 5.2.1)
- The way a user's interactions with a web page can trigger JavaScript code to change the current content of the web page, or otherwise respond to the user's activities (Section 5.2.3)

This knowledge forms the foundation for developing browser applications such as the one shown in Section 5.1. Such web pages are essentially downloadable applications that can run within a web browser without requiring additional plug-ins or "native" (to the operating system) code.

Through all this, one last aspect of the Web remains unused—and that is the Web itself. No web page is an island; any given website's usefulness and power derives at least partially from its access to/from other sites on the Internet. So far, the only connectivity mechanisms you've seen are the *link* or *anchor*—an explicit HTML tag that, when clicked, makes the web browser discard the content of its current web page and reload another page in its entirety—plus the `src` variant of the `script` tag, which causes the browser to download and run a `.js` file from the Web. Nevertheless, it is possible to communicate with the Web from *within* an individual web page, without causing the full HTML downloading-and-rendering sequence to start over. This ability, coupled with JavaScript and dynamic HTML, forms the basis of *Ajax* (Asynchronous JavaScript and XML). As with the rest of this book, we cannot cover Ajax in full detail, but this section does introduce you to its primary concepts and mechanisms.

5.3.1 Ajax in Action

To see Ajax in action, you generally need look no further than any website that claims to use "Web 2.0" technology. Scrolling maps or lists, live updates, and dynamic filters that don't change addresses or load entire new pages are very likely using Ajax to accomplish these effects. For a simple example with code that is short enough to digest easily, we've written a small Ajax-style application that you can access at `http://javascript.cs.lmu.edu/ajax-sample`.

You can use the *View Source* feature of your web browser to look at the HTML (and thus the DOM) of that sample application. To see the JavaScript code that drives this example, locate the `script` tags within the HTML source, identify the JavaScript file that is referenced by the page (the `src` attribute), and load that file into the browser (review Section 5.2.4 if you don't remember how this process works).

Take a look around the source, and note what looks familiar and what doesn't. By the end of this Ajax introduction, you should have an overall picture of how the whole thing works.

5.3.2 The Secret Ingredient: `XMLHttpRequest`

The central characteristic of an Ajax-style web page (er, *application*) is that it can send and receive new information *without* shifting from one web location to another. Dynamic HTML processes user activity and interprets it into new information to be sent back to a server on the Internet. This information, once sent, typically elicits a response from that server, usually consisting of new or updated information that must now be displayed back to the user. At this point, dynamic HTML takes over again, as the information from the server is fed back into the DOM, resulting in updates to the web page's content.

There is one catch to this connectivity: For security purposes, an Ajax application may retrieve information only *from the same server* that hosted the original Ajax web page. For example, the Ajax code in this text, which you have reached via `http://javascript.cs.lmu.edu`, can make network connections to only `http://javascript.cs.lmu.edu`. This restriction is called a *sandbox security model*—it is meant to protect you from getting web pages that make all kinds of connections to any arbitrary machine on the Internet ... behavior that, more often than not, may be quite malicious, while putting the blame squarely on *your* computer!

With this caveat in mind, let's move on to some actual code. What's the new ingredient that adds Ajax to dynamic HTML? Not surprisingly, it's "just another" built-in JavaScript object: `XMLHttpRequest`. A web browser is Ajax capable if its JavaScript environment includes `XMLHttpRequest`. A quick web search should give you an up-to-the-minute list of these browsers, although at this point, unless you're running some really old software (in computer years, not human years!), you can be quite confident that your browser—and your target users' browsers—will have `XMLHttpRequest`.

Using `XMLHttpRequest` is easy; it's figuring out *when* to use it that's trickier (more on that issue later). In fact, you can create and invoke an `XMLHttpRequest` in the usual place—a JavaScript scratch page. Type this script into our "enhanced" version at `http://javascript.cs.lmu.edu/playground`, or skip the typing by going right to `http://javascript.cs.lmu.edu/playground/ajax`:

```
// Set up some objects that everyone will want to see.
var xmlHttp;
var status = document.getElementById("status");

/*
 * This function handles changes to a request's state.
 */
```

```
var stateChanged = function() {
    var state = xmlHttp.readyState;
    switch (state) {
        case 0: status.innerHTML += "Not initialized."; break;
        case 1: status.innerHTML += "Setup"; break;
        case 2: status.innerHTML += "...Sent"; break;
        case 3: status.innerHTML += "...In Process"; break;
        case 4: status.innerHTML += "...Complete";
            // Deal with the data here.
            break;
    }
};

// This is the main script sequence.
status.innerHTML = "";
if (XMLHttpRequest) {
    xmlHttp = new XMLHttpRequest();
    xmlHttp.onreadystatechange = stateChanged;

    // We expect a URL in Input 1.
    xmlHttp.open("GET", document.getElementById("input1").value, true);
    xmlHttp.send(null);
} else {
    status.innerHTML = "Sorry, no AJAX!";
}
```

To see this script in action, type any URL that starts with `http:
//javascript.cs.lmu.edu` (because this is the site that served up the
page) into the *Input 1* text field, click *Run*, and watch the green status
area. What happens? You should see text that gradually builds up into
something like this:

Setup...Sent...In Process...In Process...In Process...Complete

You have just sent out your first Ajax-style HTTP request! Let's break the
script down to see what happened.

The script starts by declaring variables for the two objects that we'll
need later: the `XMLHttpRequest` and the `status` area on the web page. Assignment of the `status` variable is just for the sake of brevity (we don't want
to write `document.getElementById("status")` over and over again), but
we definitely need to hold on to the `XMLHttpRequest`. After the variables
comes the function `stateChanged`, followed by the main sequence.

After blanking out the status area, the script starts with this line:

```
if (XMLHttpRequest) {
```

For current browser versions, this line is a simple, elegant check for Ajax
readiness—we simply test for the presence of the built-in `XMLHttpRequest`

object. If XMLHttpRequest is defined, then the if condition evaluates to true, and we go on with our Ajax activity; otherwise, it evaluates to false, and the web page should handle the absence of Ajax in some graceful manner. In our example, the web page warns the user that Ajax is not available via the green status region.[4]

Once we know that we can "do" Ajax, the script goes ahead and creates a new object based on the XMLHttpRequest prototype. The remainder of that if block assigns one property and calls two functions. We'll look at the functions first:

open: This function defines the connection that the XMLHttpRequest object is to make. The first argument is the *method* to be used for the connection (common ones are "GET", "PUT", and "POST", but there are more); the second argument is the *URL* to access; and the third argument states whether the connection is to be asynchronous (i.e., whether to wait for it to finish before moving on). The sample script uses the "GET" method, takes whatever you typed into the *Input 1* field before running the script as the URL, and says true. Of *course*, we want an asynchronous connection: That's the first "A" in Ajax, after all.

send: This function actually initiates the connection and may include some content (its lone argument) if applicable. In the case of the sample script, we send the request with no additional information.

After xmlHttp.send(null);, the script "ends"—there is no other code to run. Seem strange? At first glance, perhaps, but don't forget that we skipped over this line:

```
xmlHttp.onreadystatechange = stateChanged;
```

This assignment, from a big-picture, structural perspective, is perhaps the most important part of the script. The onreadystatechange property is supposed to hold the JavaScript function that is to be invoked when something happens to the XMLHttpRequest object. *You* won't call this function in your own script, but the browser will. And does.

---

4. If you wish to support older browsers that are Ajax ready but use different request mechanisms, this line explodes into a near-page-long function. For brevity's sake and because older browsers will eventually fall into disuse anyway, we're leaving this more inclusive but much longer version for you to find on your own. One day this check might not even be necessary, as it may become fair to assume that *all* current browsers will be Ajax capable.

Sound familiar? *Déjà vu? Mais oui!*—onreadystatechange is an *event*. While it isn't associated with a component on the web page, the way events like onclick, onblur, and onkeyup are, onreadystatechange behaves in the same way: by setting this property, you're "setting up" the XMLHttpRequest with some code to invoke when something happens, then leaving it at that until, somewhere outside your code, the environment detects "something" happening and calls the assigned function. Thus, XMLHttpRequest is *event-driven*, just like dynamic HTML, and notification of XMLHttpRequest changes can trigger the event handler anytime after the function is assigned, just as with those unpredictable user mouse and key events.

At this point, we can finally look at the stateChanged function, which we now know to be the event handler for whenever the "ready state" of the XMLHttpRequest changes. In fact, readyState is one more property of XMLHttpRequest, as can be seen in the body of stateChanged. In this sample script, stateChanged simply displays the current value of readyState on the page's status component. You might recall the switch statement from Section 2.4.3. In this example, readyState can take on values from 0 to 4, with each value corresponding pretty much to the text shown in the script. We cumulatively build the innerHTML of the status area here, to show how an XMLHttpRequest's state progresses through its connection.

As written in this example, we never see the "not initialized" state because no event triggers stateChanged if the XMLHttpRequest weren't initialized yet. The state changes to "setup" once open is called (try the script without the send() line). We may then get more than one stateChanged invocation with readyState at "in process." When the content at the URL has been fully loaded, the state becomes "complete."

You may get multiple "in process" state change events, even though the state didn't change, because "in process" is the state during which an XMLHttpRequest is receiving data from the URL's server. Because the incoming data may be substantial, a good XMLHttpRequest implementation should keep you posted in case there are *some* data in the pipeline and your web page application might want to do something with them.

That about covers the entire sample script, as it was given. If you understand the script, you generally understand XMLHttpRequest. Once the request object does its work, and it settles into readyState === 4 (i.e., "completed," "loaded," "finished"), XMLHttpRequest's involvement technically ends. But from an Ajax perspective, there's one more thing to do, and that is ...

5.3.3 Processing Responses

You can round out the introductory Ajax script given in Section 5.3.2 by adding a line between the // Deal with the data. comment and the `break;` statement in `stateChanged`, so that the overall `case 4` arm looks like this:

```
case 4: status.innerHTML += "...Complete";
    // Deal with the data.
    document.getElementById("footer").innerHTML = xmlHttp.responseText;
    break;
```

Before running this tweaked version of the script, take a moment to think about what you would see in the playground page when you click *Run* for whatever URL you'd like to enter into the *Input 1* text field. Now actually run it. Does what happens match what you thought would happen?

In any case, that single assignment line accesses the last XMLHttp-Response property that we cover in this book: `responseText`. Simply put, this property, upon completion of an HTTP connection, holds the exact content of the server's response to the request. What we do with that content is now completely up to us.

In the sample scratch script, the content is, in all likelihood, HTML source, because you were told to provide a URL as input. This should explain what you saw—note that `responseText` was assigned directly as the `innerHTML` property of the page's `footer` component. When this property was assigned in this way, the browser tried to render this text as it would any other web page. Of course, the content probably looks nothing like what you would have seen had you accessed the URL the "normal" way, but swatches should be recognizable. There are many possible reasons for this difference, but overall it's because the content that you retrieved was meant to be viewed as a stand-alone web page, not embedded in another page's HTML.

The point here is not that you've managed to force one website's content into the page, but rather that you are free to do what you wish with the information that you receive from the server. Now that you know about `XMLHttpRequest`, you can take a closer look at the source of the fully operational Ajax example from Section 5.3.1. Specifically, find the URL that is given to the request's `open` function. If you typed that URL directly into a web browser, you should see not a web page, but plain text. This plain text, however, contains the raw information that is eventually displayed nicely on the dynamic web page.

This, then, is the final phase of a typical Ajax cycle: The server's content has been received and now resides in the request object's `responseText` property. This content can now be presented to the user in some way. In the end, `responseText` gets massaged or processed as needed, leading to some assignment to a property of a component somewhere in the DOM. If done right, this information is presented visually, the user sees this information, and his or her subsequent actions may now be based on that information.

5.3.4   Overall Ajax Structure

You may have noticed by now that an effective Ajax application can't just be "thrown together." Rather, creating one takes genuine planning, design, and discipline. To recap, a full-fledged Ajax application consists of the following main parts:

- A *model* of the data involved in the application. What information is presented initially? What new information will the user provide as he or she interacts with the web page? What updated information must be retrieved from the Web based on the user's input? How does this information translate back to the web page?

- A well-planned *view* of the application in the form of the web page that the user initially accesses. This web page must have all relevant components properly identified (via the `id` attribute in the HTML tag) for easy manipulation by JavaScript. Outgoing information comes from interactive components such as text fields, buttons, and selection lists, while incoming information can show up pretty much anywhere on the page.

- A set of JavaScript functions that effectively *control* how the application behaves. These functions determine when and how information moves from one place to another. Proper setting of event handlers in the original HTML (e.g., `onclick`, `onfocus`, `onkeyup`) helps trigger the interaction cycle by allowing the browser to call the right Java-Script code when the user does something of interest. Code triggered by these events can then either manipulate content completely locally (e.g., change the state of other controls, update their values, modify other displayed information) or seek new information from the network via `XMLHttpRequest`. When this new information arrives, code triggered by the `onreadystatechange` event handler updates the displayed content accordingly. It is this latter activity that forms the basis of what is now called Ajax-style programming.

  "Control" does not necessarily have to be user-triggered, either. Web pages that exhibit "live update" behavior without distinct browser reloads typically have ongoing activity, set up through JavaScript's built-in `setTimeout` or `setInterval` functions, that is triggered automatically at set times. This also constitutes a form of control and ultimately has the same structure: At some point, a function is called, and this function uses `XMLHttpRequest` to initiate an automatic update of the web page's content.

As you venture further into Ajax, keep this overall structure in mind. It will help to "calibrate" the decision about which technology or mechanism to use and when, while making your combined HTML and JavaScript code easier to understand and to follow.[5]

5.3.5 Where's the XML?

You might have noticed that the examples used in this section exchange plain text information to do their work—easy to read, easy to understand. But doesn't the "X" in Ajax stand for "XML," also known as eXtensible Markup Language? Yes, it does—but no, Ajax doesn't necessarily use XML. In that respect, "Ajax" is a bit of a misnomer. But it certainly sounds better than "AJAT" (text), "AJAPT" (plain text), "AJAD" (data), or any other alternative you might think up. That's just a hangup that many techies still have—we still want our cool-sounding acronyms.

For this book, we've chosen to elide the use of XML because it requires a whole bunch of additional background. The bottom line is that, in addition to plain text, Ajax-style applications can exchange any kind of information that they'd like with their servers: images, documents, and, yes, XML. The key is to choose the data format that best suits the needs of the application. XML, with its ability to represent structured, potentially complex information, is generally used when the data exchanged possesses, well, structure and complexity. But in the end, it is just one option among many for creating dynamic, information-rich, yet efficient web applications.

Chapter Summary

- Beyond `alert` and `prompt`, web pages constitute another technology that allows users to interact with JavaScript programs.

- The current web page is visible to JavaScript as the built-in `document` object, which has properties, structure, and functions just like any other JavaScript object.

- The JavaScript object representation of a web page is known as the document object model (DOM). Unlike "regular" JavaScript properties, DOM properties are frequently "hotwired" to the web page, so that modifications to those properties result in immediate changes to the web page's visible content—thus the name *dynamic HTML (DHTML)*.

- JavaScript code responds to user activity through *events*, which "hook up" user actions on web elements of interest or incoming data from network connections with the scripts that *handle* those events.

---

5. Some readers may recognize this structure and information flow as an *MVC* (model-view-controller) architecture. That's exactly what it is—if you're interested, look it up.

- JavaScript can be embedded directly into HTML code, or it can be referenced from a separate file. Both techniques use the HTML `script` tag.

- The Ajax programming style consists of DHTML combined with "in-page" access to the Web to acquire new information that was not originally a part of the page, especially information that is based on the user's input.

Exercises

1. Run the one-liners listed on page 64, making sure that you know precisely what each one does.

    (a) Identify the one-liner that has no immediate visible effect.

    (b) Identify the other one-liners that are affected by the "invisible" one. Feel free to look it up instead of figuring it out by trial and error. In either case run these one-liners in isolation to verify your answer.

2. Change the last line of the adder program on page 63 to match the following line (i.e., remove the parentheses that enclose the expression `number1 + number2`):

```
status.innerHTML = number1 + " + " + number2 + " = " +
    number1 + number2;
```

Run this new version of the adder. In what way is it different from the original version? What difference did those deleted parentheses make?

3. On most graphical user interfaces (GUIs), check boxes and radio buttons are "clickable" not only on the control itself, but also on their associated labels (e.g., when a typical native GUI displays a "☐ Do not show again" check box, then clicking on *either* the check box itself or the "Do not show again" label will toggle that control). This is not the case on web pages: By default, a check box or radio button's label does *not* respond to mouse clicks. Write an HTML/JavaScript combination that implements the standard GUI behavior for web check boxes and radio buttons.

4. Modify the scripts in Section 5.2.2 so that they turn the playground page into a basic calculator.

    (a) Write a setup script based on the one on page 64 to change the page so that the radio buttons are relabeled to say +, −, *, and /, respectively.

(b) Write the actual calculator script, based on the one on page 63, that takes two numbers from the text fields, performs the selected arithmetic operation on them, and displays the result in the green `status` area.

5. The "digit restricter" example on page 67 has a loophole for *Input 1*; it *is* possible to enter a nondigit into that field. Can you identify that loophole (i.e., which specific actions can the user take—except for running JavaScript code, of course—to make *Input 1* accept nondigit characters)?

6. If you play with the "box dragger" example (referenced on page 69 and available from `http://javascript.cs.lmu.edu/boxes`) for a long enough time, you will notice that it isn't quite perfect. Sometimes, drag operations "abort" and leave the boxes in an inconsistent state.

(a) Experiment with this example a little bit. Can you identify one possible explanation for this behavior?

(b) How might you be able to resolve this issue?

(c) Code your idea to see if it works.

7. Implement a simple "make change" web application. The application should consist of an HTML file with an input field requesting an amount from which to make change and a *Make Change* button. Clicking the button should display, below the text field, the number of quarters, dimes, nickels, and pennies needed for the amount given by the user. The JavaScript that provides this functionality should be stored in a separate `.js` file; the only JavaScript that is directly included in the HTML file should be the event handlers needed to deliver the requested functionality.

8. At what point in an `XMLHttpRequest` object's life cycle would its `readyState` property be 0, or "not initialized?" Write a JavaScript program that shows this.

9. The script from page 76 is tweaked on page 79 so that you can see text or HTML content that is retrieved by the `XMLHttpRequest` in the footer of the scratch page. But this content is not necessarily HTML or plain text; it can really be anything that is downloadable from the Web. Modify the playground page and/or JavaScript to accommodate responses that hold *image* data.

10. The Ajax sandbox security model pertains to code that has been downloaded from the Web; code that resides as a file on your machine (i.e., opened through a web browser's *File | Open* command) can connect to anything.

(a) Save the scratch page at `http://javascript.cs.lmu.edu/playground` as an HTML file on your own machine, and then open it in your web browser. Type and run the script from page 76 and try accessing URLs other than those that start with `http://javascript.cs.lmu.edu/`. What happens, compared to doing the same thing directly from `http://javascript.cs.lmu.edu/playground`?

(b) Why do you think local files are "exempt" from the sandbox?

11. Read the source code of `http://javascript.cs.lmu.edu/ajax-sample` to answer the following questions:

(a) What does the URL invoked by the application's `XMLHttpRequest` look like (i.e., what is its format)?

(b) Try to visit URLs of this format directly from your web browser. What happens?

12. Write a completely different web page that performs the same task as the one at `http://javascript.cs.lmu.edu/ajax-sample`, but has a look and feel that is all your own. Make sure to accommodate the fact that this web page will be provided by a different machine (such as locally on your computer) while still using the same server for `XMLHttpRequest`s.

A s we reach the end of this book, you might have noticed that we both started *and* finished the text with an introduction. First, we introduced you to JavaScript as a programming language; eventually, we capped things off with an introduction to Ajax, an extremely powerful application of JavaScript enabling truly interactive software delivered over the Web. This is, of course, by design: With all worthwhile subjects, there are no real endpoints, just transitions to other (deeper, broader) areas. You started by seeing JavaScript as a pure programming language, without the distractions or hype that accompany technology bandwagons and trends. In the end, presumably with a better grasp of the language, you find yourself at the cusp of using JavaScript to implement a class of applications that has already transformed the way many people use the World Wide Web, and whose full potential has yet to be realized.

So where do you go from here? Presuming that we've gotten your attention and interest with this little volume, the trite answer of "anywhere" actually isn't that far off. We certainly did not cover all of the JavaScript language (a much longer book would be required for that!), nor did we mention the many professional JavaScript libraries used in the real world today. Instead, we sometimes used phrases such as "beyond the scope of this book," or "leave the details to you." Those are good places to start: Find something that made you wish it were covered, find information that goes into deeper detail in those areas, and try to apply that information.

- If you are interested in the JavaScript language, pick up a language reference, where you'll encounter advanced and powerful features such as exceptions, reflection, enumeration, and something called "duck typing." Learn more about closures and regular expressions. Find out about labeled statements, the `typeof` operator, the `constructor` property, and the mysterious and much-maligned `eval` function. Several built-in objects, such as `Number` and `String` (and their prototypes), have properties you might find useful. For the exceptionally curious, pore through the reference to answer questions such as "Why don't I see `isPrototypeOf` when iterating through my object's properties?" and "Why can't I delete the `constructor` property from `Object.prototype`?"

■ If you are interested in developing expertise in JavaScript *programming* to further your career goals, familiarize yourself with JavaScript tools and libraries, as well as related technologies such as HTML, XML, and JSON. While tools do come and go, we think it is a safe bet that (the indispensible) JSLint [Cro02] and the (Firefox-specific) Firebug will be viable as long as JavaScript itself is viable.

Wherever your interests lie, we're happy to have given you the dual introductions in this brief book. May you find yourself with the confidence, skills, and ability to introduce *yourself* to more knowledge on your own.

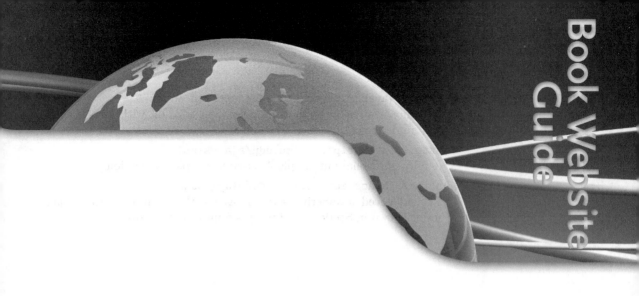

ample web pages and code are an integral part of getting the most out of this book. Here's a list of what's available at `http://javascript.cs.lmu.edu`:

- `http://javascript.cs.lmu.edu/scratch`
  A rudimentary JavaScript scratch page, best used for learning the language and introductory scripts.

- `http://javascript.cs.lmu.edu/scratch/phrase-to-phone`
  The rudimentary JavaScript scratch page, with the introductory script shown in Section 1.3 pretyped into the text area.

- `http://javascript.cs.lmu.edu/phone-to-phrase`
  The rudimentary JavaScript scratch page, with the script shown in Section 1.4 pretyped into the text area.

- `http://javascript.cs.lmu.edu/phone-form`
  A full dynamic HTML front end for the script introduced in Section 1.3, plus some additional functionality facilitated by the language features covered in Chapters 2 through 5.

- `http://javascript.cs.lmu.edu/js/phoneConversion.js`
  Supporting JavaScript file that defines the core functionality behind the `http://javascript.cs.lmu.edu/phone-form` application.

- `http://javascript.cs.lmu.edu/playground`
  A more advanced JavaScript scratch page, including assorted HTML elements for learning dynamic HTML and possibly some Ajax.

- `http://javascript.cs.lmu.edu/boxes`
  A demonstration page showing dynamic HTML mouse event handling.

- `http://javascript.cs.lmu.edu/deferred`
  A demonstration page showing deferred execution with `setTimeout` and `setInterval`.
- `http://javascript.cs.lmu.edu/ajax-sample`
  A fully functional but simple Ajax-style sample application.
- `http://javascript.cs.lmu.edu/playground/ajax`
  The advanced JavaScript scratch page with the introductory Ajax script shown in Section 5.3.2 pretyped into the text area.

Ajax An acronym for *Asynchronous JavaScript and XML*, which is a style of JavaScript web programming where requests are made to a server and where responses, generally but not necessarily in XML, are processed at some later time without leaving the current web page.

Array A collection of values, indexed from 0. A true JavaScript array has a `length` property that, if assigned a value by a script, will expand or shrink the array.

Character A named symbol, such as PLUS SIGN, MUSICAL SYMBOL F CLEF, CHEROKEE LETTER QUV, or WHITE CHESS KNIGHT. Do not confuse a character with a *glyph*, which is a picture of a character. For example, the two distinct letters LATIN CAPITAL LETTER P and CYRILLIC CAPITAL LETTER ER can both be represented with the glyph P; similarly, the distinct characters GREEK CAPITAL LETTER SIGMA and N-ARY SUMMATION can both be represented with the glyph Σ.

Character Set A collection of characters, each of which is tagged with a unique integer called its *codepoint*. For example, in the Unicode Character Set, the character CYRILLIC SMALL LETTER YU has codepoint 44E (hex). Popular character sets in use today are Unicode, ASCII, and ISO-8859-1.

Constructor A function that creates a new object.

DOM An acronym for *document object model*, which represents the structure and content of a web page as a JavaScript object.

Event An action such as a page load, button press, or keystroke, to which a script may wish to respond.

Expression A chunk of code that is evaluated.

Function Code that can be called, generally with arguments. JavaScript, unlike some languages, treats functions as values that can be assigned to variables and passed as arguments to other functions.

Loop A chunk of code that is performed multiple times, until some condition becomes true (or false—but if you think about it, that's pretty much the same thing).

Object A value made up of named properties.

Prototype An object holding properties intended to be shared by a number of similar objects.

Script A sequence of statements intended to be executed as a single unit.

Statement A unit of execution within a script. The JavaScript statements are the empty statement, variable declaration, evaluation, block, `if`, `for`, `while`, `continue`, `break`, `return`, `with`, `switch`, `throw`, and `try`.

String A text value. Strings can be viewed as a sequence of symbols or characters. Thus they have length, and individual characters in the string can be accessed by a numeric index starting from zero.

Type A particular set of values. All values in JavaScript belong to one of six types: undefined, null, Boolean, number, string, or object.

Unicode An internationally standardized character set, containing hundreds of thousands of characters. It is the native character set of JavaScript.

Variable A named "container" for a value. The variable can be updated by assigning it a new value.

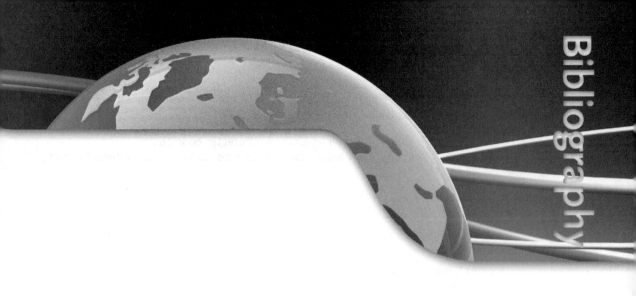

[Cro01] Douglas Crockford. Javascript: The world's most misunderstood programming language. `http://javascript.crockford.com/javascript.html`, 2001. Accessed May 24, 2008.

[Cro02] Douglas Crockford. JSLint: The JavaScript verifier. `http://www.jslint.com/`, 2002. Accessed August 4, 2008.

[Cro08a] Douglas Crockford. *JavaScript: The good parts*. O'Reilly Media, 2008.

[Cro08b] Douglas Crockford. JavaScript: The world's most misunderstood programming language has become the world's most popular programming language. `http://javascript.crockford.com/popular.html`, 2008. Accessed May 24, 2008.

[ECM99] ECMA. *Standard ECMA-262, ECMAScript language specification*, 3rd edition. ECMA International, December 1999. `http://www.ecma-international.org/publications/standards/Ecma-262.htm`.

[Fla06] David Flanagan. *JavaScript: The definitive guide*, 5th edition. O'Reilly Media, 2006.

[Sco05] Michael L. Scott. *Programming language pragmatics*. Morgan Kaufmann, 2005.

[Spo06] Joel Spolsky. Can your programming language do this? `http://www.joelonsoftware.com/items/2006/08/01.html`, 2006. Accessed May 31, 2008.

[Uni06] The Unicode Consortium. *The unicode standard, version 5.0.* Addison-Wesley Professional, 2006.

[Uni08] Unicode, Inc. The Unicode character code charts. `http://www.unicode.org/charts`, 2008. Accessed June 13, 2008.